EYEWITNESS TRAVEL

TOP10
CHICAGO

ELAINE GLUSAC
ELISA KRONISH
ROBERTA SOTONOFF

Penguin
Random
House

Top 10 Chicago Highlights

The Top 10 of Everything

CONTENTS

Chicago Area by Area

Streetsmart

Within each Top 10 list in this book, no hierarchy of quality or popularity is implied. All 10 are, in the editor's opinion, of roughly equal merit.

Throughout this book, floors are referred to in accordance with American usage; i.e. the "first floor" is at ground level.

Front cover and spine Tour boat in downtown Chicago near Michigan Avenue Bridge
Back cover The Neo-Classical building housing the Museum of Science and Industry
Title page The iconic clock outside Macy's and the Chicago Theatre behind on N. State Street

Welcome to
Chicago

Chicago has been called the "City of the Big Shoulders" for its industrial brawn, the "Second City" for its size, and the "Windy City" for its politics – all of which the city embraces with good-humored warmth, confidence, and imagination. With Eyewitness Top 10 Chicago, it's yours to explore.

The city's own motto is "urbs in horto," or city in a garden, and its connection to nature is readily apparent, from the vast Lake Michigan shoreline to the Chicago River that divides the city. Its public living room is art-filled **Millennium Park**, and its playground is **Navy Pier**, jutting into the lake with carnival-like attractions as well as more high-minded distractions such as the Chicago Shakespeare Theater. Both the **Lincoln Park Zoo** and the **John G. Shedd Aquarium** offer exposure to natural life beyond the region.

Culture abounds indoors and out. Birthplace of the skyscraper, Chicago has a range of architecture spanning the lofty **Willis Tower** and the earth-grounded Prairie School homes of Frank Lloyd Wright in **Oak Park**. Museums are similarly diverse, from the **Art Institute of Chicago**, stocked with treasures bestowed by civic-minded 19th-century collectors, to the natural history curiosities of the **Field Museum** and the scientific wonders of the **Museum of Science and Industry**. The arts come alive nightly in more than 200 theaters and many jazz and blues clubs in town.

Whether you are visiting for a weekend or longer, our Top 10 guide distills the best of Chicago, from the hidden neighborhood pub to the bustling **Magnificent Mile**. There are tips for the best freebies and tours, places to take the kids and dine memorably, plus seven easy-to-follow itineraries, designed to make the most use of your time in the city. Add inspiring photography and detailed maps, and you've got the essential pocket-sized travel companion. **Enjoy the book, and enjoy Chicago.**

Clockwise from top: Chicago skyline; lion statues outside the Art Institute of Chicago; Sue, the *Tyrannosaurus rex* exhibit at the Field Museum; Arthur Heurtley House, Oak Park; window at the Richard H. Driehaus Gallery of Stained Glass; Jay Pritzker Pavilion, Millennium Park; Botanic Garden

Exploring Chicago

Thanks to a convenient concentration of attractions, it is easy to cram Chicago's highlights into a few days, or even a weekend. The following two- and four-day itineraries are packed with ideas for you to make the most of your visit, and to fully immerse yourself in the city's sights, sounds, and flavors.

Magnificent Mile is a great, bustling shopping experience.

Two Days in Chicago

Day ❶

MORNING

Take a **Chicago Architecture Foundation** cruise *(see p115)* along the Chicago River to get an overview of the city's design prowess. Walk a few blocks south to explore **Millennium Park** *(see pp34–5)*.

AFTERNOON

Take the bridge from the park to the **Art Institute of Chicago** *(see pp14–17)* to admire the Impressionist collection. See the city on high from nearby **Willis Tower** *(see pp12–13)*, indulge in pizza at **Uno's** *(see p61)*, and then catch a comedy show at **Second City** *(see p55)*.

Day ❷

MORNING

Start your day with a visit to the **John G. Shedd Aquarium** *(see pp28–9)* – if you book online in advance you can skip the line. Afterward, cross the Museum Campus to the famous **Field Museum** *(see pp18–19)*.

AFTERNOON

Make your way to **Navy Pier** *(see pp24–5)* for a whirl on some of the carnival rides. Then hit retail magnet, **Magnificent Mile** *(see pp32–3)*. Finish up at a jazz or blues club *(see pp56–7)*.

Four Days in Chicago

Day ❶

MORNING

Sign up for the **Chicago Architecture Foundation** *(see p115)* river cruise and disembark at Michigan Avenue. Walk up the **Magnificent Mile** *(see pp32–3)* to take in the pulse of the city.

AFTERNOON

After lunch at **Spiaggia** *(see p83)*, continue northward for a stroll in the leafy **Lincoln Park Zoo** *(see pp30–31)*.

Day ❷

MORNING

Browse the vast collections of the **Art Institute of Chicago** *(see pp14–15)*. Take the bridge from the Modern Wing into **Millennium Park** *(see pp34–5)*, and grab lunch at **Park Grill** *(see pp34–5)*.

Aviation exhibit at the **Museum of Science and Industry**

Willis Tower is the tallest building in Chicago.

Key
— Two-day itinerary
— Four-day itinerary

Navy Pier is a leisure playground for all ages.

AFTERNOON
Take a trip on the CTA Green Line "L" out to **Oak Park** (see pp36–7) to see architect Frank Lloyd Wright's former home and studio. On the return, get off in the Loop to hit one of the many restaurants and bars in the area (see p77).

Day ❸
MORNING
Start at the **John G. Shedd Aquarium** (see pp28–9), then cross the Museum Campus to marvel at Sue, the giant *Tyrannosaurus rex* on display at the **Field Museum** (see pp18–19).

AFTERNOON
Admire the city from aloft at the **Willis Tower** (see pp12–13). Then visit **Navy Pier** (see pp24–5) for a lake cruise, dinner, and a performance at **Chicago Shakespeare Theater** (see pp25 & 55).

Day ❹
MORNING
Spend the morning exploring the many exhibits of the **Museum of Science and Industry** (see pp20–21) in Hyde Park, including the coal mine and German WWII submarine.

AFTERNOON
Have lunch at **Valois** cafeteria (see p105), then take the Metra train to **Millennium Park** (see pp34–5). Rent a Divvy bicycle and ride the **Lakefront Recreational Path** (see p64). After dark, stroll around the illuminated **Buckingham Fountain** (see p72).

Top 10 Chicago Highlights

The futuristic Jay Pritzker Pavilion in Millennium Park

🔟 Chicago Highlights

Big-city sophistication combined with small-town hospitality create the perfect blend in this, the Midwest's largest city. Chicago's architecture, cuisine for all budgets and taste, great shopping, diverse ethnic neighborhoods, outstanding museums, and a lakefront setting make this an exciting place to visit.

① Willis Tower and Its Views

The city's skyscraping superlative is actually made up of nine tube-like sections. The views are awesome: on a clear day, you can see up to 40 miles (64 km) from the 103rd-floor Skydeck *(see pp12–13)*.

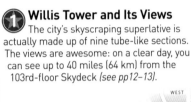

② The Art Institute of Chicago

This grande dame of Chicago's art scene features world-renowned collections. The Impressionist section is outstanding *(see pp14–17)*.

③ Field Museum

Delve into cultures and environments from ancient Egypt to modern Africa, via Midwestern wildlife, and the underground life of bugs. The Field also offers a closeup of the world's largest and most complete *Tyrannosaurus rex* skeleton *(see pp18–19)*.

④ Museum of Science and Industry

This museum is the only building left from the 1893 World's Columbian Exposition. Interactive exhibits range from space exploration to coal mining, including a ride on the Silver Streak train *(see pp20–21)*.

5 Navy Pier
Once a tourist trap, this Lake Michigan pier is now a bustling year-round playground. In warm weather, take a boat tour or join the throngs that stroll along the pier and get some amazing city views *(see pp24–5)*.

John G. Shedd Aquarium 6
Chicago's aquarium on the lakefront houses thousands of marine animals, from big beluga whales to tiny seahorses. Get a fish-eye view at the Oceanarium's underwater viewing galleries *(see pp28–9)*.

7 Lincoln Park Zoo
It might not be the biggest but it's one of the oldest zoos in the country. Kids love the viewing gallery at the Polar Bear Pool and the AT&T Endangered Species Carousel *(see pp30–31)*.

8 Magnificent Mile
Chicago's premier shopping destination is a four-lane stretch of North Michigan Avenue. It also claims two of only a few structures to survive the 1871 Great Chicago Fire *(see pp32–3)*.

9 Millennium Park
Opened in 2004, Millennium Park has many attractions that are a magnet for locals and visitors alike *(see pp34–5)*.

10 Frank Lloyd Wright's Oak Park
Frank Lloyd Wright, creator of Prairie Style architecture, was based in this Chicago suburb for 20 years. His legacy is an "outdoor museum" of 25 buildings. Take a self-guided or guided tour of his creations *(see pp36–7)*.

TOP 10 ⭐ Willis Tower and Its Views

It might have lost the US's tallest building slot, but Willis Tower is still the second tallest in the country, at 1,450 ft (442 m). Designed by Chicago firm Skidmore, Owings & Merrill, the tower uses nine exterior frame tubes, avoiding the need for interior supports. For awesome 360-degree views of the city, head to the 103rd-floor Skydeck, where the brave can also step into a series of glass boxes that provide fascinating views straight down to the ground.

1 John Hancock Center

The Willis Tower's North Side counterpart is this 100-story skyscraper. It houses a retail area, offices, and apartments – as well as an open-air observatory (see p79).

2 Soldier Field

Home to the Chicago Bears football team (see p67) for over 30 years, the lakeside stadium **(above)**, which opened in 1924, saw the addition of a 67,000-seat structure in 2003.

3 Marina City

When built in 1964, these 60-story buildings **(left)**, nicknamed the corncobs, were once the tallest residential structures in the world (see p42).

4 Chicago River

Chicago's 156-mile- (250-km-) long river tops world records with its 43 opening bridges. An amazing engineering feat resulted in the reversal of the river flow in 1900 *(see p40)*. Every St. Patrick's Day the main branch is dyed green.

7 Lake Michigan

This is the third largest of the five Great Lakes. Water temperatures struggle to hit tepid during summer, but many beach-goers swim nevertheless. On a clear day, you can often see across to the shores of Indiana and Michigan.

TOP 10 TOWER FACTS

1 It is 110 stories high
2 It weighs a massive 222,500 tons
3 The tower took three years to construct
4 Building costs topped $150 million
5 It contains over 2,000 miles (3,220 km) of electric cables …
6 … And 25,000 miles (40,233 km) of piping
7 25,000 people enter and exit each day
8 1.3 million visit the Skydeck each year
9 The elevators travel at an ear-popping 1,600 ft (490 m) per minute
10 Six automatic machines wash its 16,100 windows

Willis Tower dominating the Chicago skyline

9 McCormick Place

The first convention center opened here in 1960 but burned down seven years later. Helmut Jahn built the second in 1971 at twice the size with 40,000 sprinkler heads. Four buildings now make up this complex, and are connected by a shop-lined promenade.

5 United Center

This vast indoor sports arena and concert venue is also known as "the house that Michael built," as it was basketball player Michael Jordan's fame that attracted the money to fund it. Outside, there's a statue of him.

8 Merchandise Mart

One of the world's largest commercial buildings (in floor area), this 1930s structure was run by the Kennedy family until the late 1990s *(see p79)*.

10 Navy Pier

A former naval base turned fun-filled mecca, and Chicago's top attraction *(see pp24–5)*.

6 Grant Park

Built entirely on landfill following the Great Chicago Fire *(see p40)*, this 319-acre park **(right)** is one of the city's largest and the site of summer music festivals *(see p46)*.

The Art Institute of Chicago

Guarded by iconic lions and up a flight of grand stone steps is the Midwest's largest art museum. Housed in a massive Beaux-Arts edifice with an impressive Modern Wing by Renzo Piano, the Institute has some 260,000 works from around the globe, and is famous for its Impressionist and Post-Impressionist collections.

3 Nighthawks
One of the best-known images in 20th-century American art, this 1942 painting **(left)** by Realist Edward Hopper has a melancholy quality. It includes a depiction of fluorescent lighting, new at the time to US cities.

1 Acrobats at the Cirque Fernando
Children were often the subjects of Renoir's sunny paintings: this luminous 1879 work shows a circus owner's daughters taking a bow after their act.

4 The Old Guitarist
A young, struggling Picasso painted this tortured 1903 portrait during his Blue Period. It reflected his grief over a friend's suicide and was a precursor to his own style of Cubism.

American Gothic 2
Grant Wood borrowed from the detailed style of Flemish Renaissance art to create this painting (1930). Though perceived by many as satirical, the painting **(right)** celebrates rural American values.

5 Stacks of Wheat Series
From 1890 to 1891, Monet painted 30 views of the haystacks that stood outside his house in France. This museum has six, which illustrate the Impressionist doctrine of capturing the fleeting effects of light in nature.

NEED TO KNOW

MAP L4 ■ 111 S. Michigan Ave ■ "L" Station: Adams (Green, Orange, Purple, Brown & Pink lines), Monroe (Blue & Red lines) ■ 312-443-3600 ■ www.artic.edu

Open 10:30am–5pm Mon–Fri (to 8pm Thu); 10:30am–5pm Sat & Sun

Adm: adults $25; students, seniors and children 14 yrs and older $19; under-14s free; free adm 1st and 2nd Wed of month, 5–8pm Thu, 5–9pm summer, and Feb ■ DA

■ Terzo Piano (Modern Wing) is perfect for a fine-dining lunch with city views, or cross over to GePaDe Caffe (60 E. Adams St.) for great panini.

■ Join a free, hour-long introductory tour. Meet in gallery 100 (noon daily, and 2pm Tue, Wed, and Fri).

■ Don't miss the reconstruction of the 1893 Stock Exchange Trading Room.

Museum Guide

The Art Institute is the second-largest art museum in the US. Locations of works and accessibility of specific galleries are subject to change; if there is a particular work you want to see, check in advance to ensure it is on view.

6 At the Moulin Rouge

Unlike many of his fellow Impressionists who painted serene scenes, Toulouse-Lautrec was drawn to the exuberant nightlife of Paris. This dramatic painting (1892) celebrates the Moulin Rouge cabaret **(above)**.

8 America Windows

Unveiled at the Art Institute in 1977, Marc Chagall's stunning stained-glass windows were a gift to the city he loved. The six vibrant panels depict the US as a place of cultural and religious freedom.

10 The Herring Net

Winslow Homer honed his Realist skills as an illustrator for magazines. After moving to Maine, he created a series of images, including this one (1885), depicting man's complex relationship with the sea.

7 A Sunday on La Grande Jatte – 1884

Massive and mesmerizing, this painting took Georges Seurat two years to complete. The scene is created from dots of color, based on his study of optical theory, later known as pointillism.

9 The Child's Bath

The only American to exhibit in Paris with the Impressionists, Mary Cassatt often portrayed women and children as in this **(left)**, her most famous painting (1893). Her domestic subjects reflect the limited freedom of women at the time.

Key to Floorplan

▨ Lower level
▨ First level
▨ Second level
▨ Third level

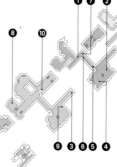

🔟 Collections

Two Sisters, by Pierre August Renoir, a highlight of the European Collection

① European Collection

Arranged chronologically, and spanning the Middle Ages through 1950, this prodigious collection includes a significant array of Renaissance and Baroque art and sculpture. However, its main draw is a body of nearly 400 Impressionist and Post-Impressionist paintings. Instrumental in its creation was Bertha Honoré Palmer who acquired over 40 Impressionist works (largely ignored in France at the time) for the 1893 World's Columbian Exposition.

② American Arts

This impressive holding contains some 5,500 paintings and sculptures dating from the colonial period to 1950. In addition, paintings and works on paper are on loan from the Terra collection, and there is a range of decorative arts, including furniture, glass, and ceramics from the 18th century through to the present. The silver collection is especially noteworthy.

③ Arthur Rubloff Collection of Paperweights

This fabulous and unusual assemblage numbers in excess of 1,400 paperweights, making it one of the largest of its kind in the world. It showcases colorful and exquisite examples from all periods, designs, and techniques. The paperweights mostly originate from 19th-century France, though some were made in America and the United Kingdom. Displays also reveal the secrets of how paperweights are made.

Arthur Rubloff paperweight

④ African and Amerindian Art

A wide variety of artifacts, including sculptures, ceramics, furniture, textiles, masks, jewelry, beadwork, and metalwork, make up this relatively small, but interesting

African and Amerindian exhibits

collection. Exhibits from both continents are arranged by region and culture: ceremonial and ritual objects are particularly intriguing.

5 Architecture

Given the city's strong architectural heritage and focus, it is not surprising that Chicago's Art Institute boasts an architecture and design department, one of only a few in the US. Sketches and drawings are accessible by appointment, and changing public displays feature models, drawings, and architectural pieces, such as a stained-glass window by Frank Lloyd Wright.

6 Modern and Contemporary Art

This important collection represents the significant art movements in Europe and the US from 1950 to the present day, including a strong body of Surrealist works, and paintings by Picasso, Matisse, and Kandinsky, as well as showing how American artists, such as Georgia O'Keeffe, interpreted European Modernism.

7 Thorne Miniature Rooms

Narcissa Ward Thorne, a Chicago art patron, combined her love of miniatures with her interest in interiors and decorative arts to create the 68 rooms in this unique Lilliputian installation. Some of the 1 inch:1 foot scale rooms are replicas of specific historic interiors, while others are

Museum Floorplan

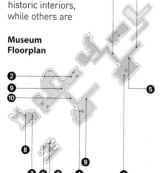

One of Thorne's miniature rooms

period recreations, combining features copied from a variety of sites or based on illustrations and other records of period furniture.

8 Photography

Spanning the history of the medium, from its origins in 1839 to the present, this eminent collection was started by Georgia O'Keeffe in 1949 with the donation of works by Alfred Stieglitz. Many modern masters, including Julien Levy, Edward Weston, Paul Strand, and Eugène Atget, are represented.

9 Asian Art

This sizeable collection covers 5,000 years and features Chinese ceramics and jades, Japanese screens, and Southeast Asian sculpture. The museum's assemblage of Japanese woodblock prints, such as *Courtesan* (c.1705–1715) by Kaigetsudo Dohan, is one of the most impressive outside Japan. Look out, too, for the rare early 14th-century scroll painting, *Legends of the Yuzu Nembutsu Sect*.

10 Arms and Armor

The Harding Collection of Arms and Armor is one of the largest in America. On permanent display are over 200 items related to the art of war, including weapons, and complete and partial suits of armor for men – as well as horses. The items displayed originate from Europe, the United States, and the Middle East, and date from the 15th through the 19th centuries.

TOP 10 ⭐ Field Museum

Founded in 1893 to display items from the World's Columbian Exposition, and renamed in 1905 to honor its first major benefactor, Marshall Field, this vast museum offers fascinating insights into global cultures and environments past and present. Home to all sorts of cultural treasures, fossils, and artifacts, as well as to myriad interactive exhibits, make no bones about it: this natural history museum is one of the best in the country.

Sue ①

A *Tyrannosaurus rex* (right), 13-ft (4-m) high by 42-ft (12.8-m) long – the largest, most complete, and best preserved ever found. Her real 600-lb (272-kg) skull is on view nearby.

② Crown Family PlayLab

Six themed areas, from a scientist's lab to a dinosaur dig, are full of things for kids to discover.

③ Grainger Hall of Gems

Fiber-optic lighting magically illuminates over 500 glittering gems, precious stones, and minerals. Even though it's a replica, the star of the show is the breathtaking Hope Diamond (left).

NEED TO KNOW

MAP L6 ■ 1400 S. Lake Shore Dr. ■ Metra station: Roosevelt Rd. ■ 312-922-9410 ■ www.fieldmuseum.org

Open 9am–5pm daily

Adm: adults $22, children (3–11) $15, seniors and students with ID $19 ■ DA

■ Grab a bite to eat under the watchful gaze of dinosaur Sue at the Corner Bakery (main level).

■ Two free trolley services link the Field, the Shedd (*see pp28–9*), and the Art Institute (*see pp16–17*) with the nearest Metra and CTA stations and downtown.

■ Have a museum-related question? Look out for attendants carrying a big "Ask Me" sign.

Museum Guide

The main entrance is located on the museum's north side, though visitors typically enter on the south, where buses, trolleys, and cabs drop off. A third (first level) west entrance is suitable for wheelchair access. If you visit on a weekday, it's worth asking staff about the museum's Free Highlights Tours, which take place twice daily. And don't forget to look for information on the day's special events, tours, and activities, posted throughout the building.

4 Inside Ancient Egypt

This part-original, part-replica Egyptian ruin leads you up and down stairs, into Egyptian bedrooms and tombs, and through a market-place. See how Cleopatra lived and how mummies were wrapped.

Africa 7

Browse the wares of a Saharan market, experience life on a slave ship, and see a pair of fighting elephants: this exhibit offers an amazing and educational journey through ancient and modern Africa for all ages **(right)**.

8 Pacific Spirits

A celebration of vibrant Pacific islander culture: visitors can see dramatic masks, listen to recorded sounds from the swamps of New Guinea, and bang on an impressive 9-ft (3-m) drum.

9 Evolving Planet

Journey through four billion years of life on Earth as a wide range of displays tell the story of evolution. Interact with single-celled organisms, giant dinosaurs, and our first human ancestors.

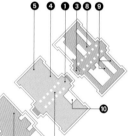

Key to Floorplan
- First level
- Main level
- Upper level

5 Lions of Tsavo

In 1898, these two partners in crime killed and ate 140 men who were constructing a bridge in Kenya, before they in turn were hunted and killed. The skins were first used as rugs, before being mounted as you see today.

Underground Adventure 6

Enter this larger-than-life "subterranean" ecosystem to get a bug's-eye view of life. Wander through a jungle of roots **(right)**, and listen to the chatter of a busy ant colony. Extra admission charged.

10 The Ancient Americas

Step into the world of Ice Age mammoth-hunters, enter an 800-year-old pueblo, and explore the Aztec Empire, as artifacts **(left)** and displays uncover 13,000 years of human history in the Americas.

Museum of Science and Industry

The cultural star of the city's Far South, this museum was the first in North America to introduce interactive exhibits, with a record of innovative, hands-on displays dating back to the 1930s. More than one million visitors flock annually to this vast Neo-Classical building, which houses more than 800 exhibits and is a Chicago must-see, especially for families. Make sure you arrive rested, since it takes a whole day to hit just the top attractions.

1 Henry Crown Space Center

This, the first manned spacecraft to orbit the moon, offers a peek into the 1960s space race. Historic photos, space suits, and a training module set the scene.

2 Science Storms

This two-story exhibit **(above)** illustrates basic principles of physics and chemistry using recreations of natural phenomena, including a 40-ft (12-m) tornado, a giant Tesla coil that produces lighting, and a 30-ft (9-m) wave tank.

3 Coal Mine

Venture down a simulated 600 ft (184 m) in an authentic shaft elevator to discover how coal was extracted in the 1930s compared to today. The mini train ride enhances the underground illusion.

4 Omnimax Theater

The films shown in this five-story theater make the viewers feel like they are right in the thick of the on-screen action and adventures. On a rotating program, the films are screened approximately every 50 minutes.

5 YOU! The Experience

Discover aspects of the human body and mind from a new perspective. The centerpiece of this exhibit is the giant 13-ft- (4-m-) tall animated 3-D human heart, which offers a fascinating interactive experience.

7 ToyMaker 3000

Twelve robotic arms work the assembly line to produce toy top after colorful top in this display of computer integrated manufacturing technology. Race a robot to see who can trace letters faster, and souvenir tops come free.

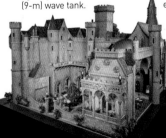

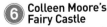

6 Colleen Moore's Fairy Castle

Star of the silent screen, Colleen Moore commissioned the design of this lavish miniature castle, a study in craftsmanship **(left)**, and lovingly filled it with over 2,000 one-twelfth-scaled objects, including the world's smallest Bible.

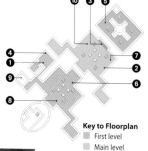

8 All Aboard the Silver Streak
Both Art Deco design aficionados and rail buffs are drawn to this streamlined, vintage Zephyr train **(above)** with its ground-breaking diesel-electric engine.

Key to Floorplan
■ First level
■ Main level
■ Upper level

10 The Great Train Story
Over 20 miniature trains race past skyscrapers, through prairies, and over the Rockies to the Pacific Docks on 1,425 ft (437 m) of track **(above)** that replicate the 2,200-mile (3,540-km) train trip from Chicago to Seattle on this interactive model railroad.

9 U-505 Submarine
Take a tour around this original 1941 German U-boat **(above)**. The submarine was captured during World War II and still looks much as it did then, complete with an Enigma codebreaking machine.

NEED TO KNOW

MAP F6 ■ 57th St. & Lake Shore Dr. ■ Metra station: 55th/56th/57th Sts. ■ 1-773-684-1414 ■ www.msichicago.org

Open 9:30am–4pm daily

Adm: adults $18, children (3–11) $11, seniors $14; including one Omnimax show: adults $27, children $18, seniors $21 ■ DA

■ The Brain Food Court serves above-average fare, and has a kids' zone.

■ Advance tickets reserved on the Internet or telephone cost extra but are worth it on busy weekends.

■ Additional Omnimax tickets are sold at all museum entrances: adults $8, children (3–11) $6, seniors $7.

Museum Guide
The museum has two main entrances – the Great Hall (first level) and the Henry Crown Space Center (for the Omnimax Theater). Head first to tour-only displays (Silver Streak, U-505, the Coal Mine) as later waits for these can be more than an hour. Visit the Omnimax later – you'll appreciate sitting down. Strollers can be rented in the Great Hall.

TOP10 Exhibits

Transportation Gallery

1 Transportation Gallery
A full-size Boeing 727 and a British World War II fighter plane dangle dramatically above a steam locomotive and the world's fastest land vehicle, while visitors explore the forces of flight via engaging computer games and videos.

2 U-505
Artifacts, archival footage, and interactive challenges bring to life this restored U-505 German submarine. Optional on-board tours of the boat are available.

3 Genetics and the Baby Chick Hatchery
Explore the complex and controversial world of genetics and genetic engineering and learn how cloning is possible, while viewing real cloned mice.

4 Farm Tech
Learn about life on today's farms and the modern technologies that get food from the field to your table. Children can ride in a real combine and take part in a cow-milking challenge.

5 Networld
The world of cyberspace comes alive here via educational yet fun hands-on displays.

6 The Art of the Bicycle
This fascinating exhibit explores the pioneering evolution of the bicycle over the last 200 years.

7 Ships Through the Ages
Here, model ships chart marine transportation from Egyptian sailboats through to modern ocean liners. Highlights include scale versions of Christopher Columbus's three ships.

8 The Swiss Jolly Ball
The world's largest pinball machine has been here since 1998. Watch the pinball race through Swiss-themed scenery and admire its complicated mechanics.

9 Communications Zone
The Whispering Gallery shows how sound waves make the faintest whisper audible at the other end of a room, while THINK explores the working relationship between people and technology.

10 Poop Happens
In this one-of-a-kind science theater show, viewers follow food right the way through the digestive process, from the mouth to the stomach – and beyond.

Museum Floorplan

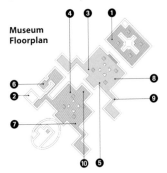

THE MUSEUM'S ORIGINS

Ferris Wheel

Built as the Palace of Fine Arts in 1893, the Museum of Science and Industry is the only building left from Daniel Burnham's "White City." This was built for the World's Columbian Exposition, marking the 400th anniversary (albeit one year late) of Christopher Columbus's arrival in the New World. Burnham, the Director of Works for the fair *(see p43)*, commissioned architects like Charles Atwood to create structures that would showcase the best in design, culture, and technology. The Field Museum *(see pp18–19)* inhabited the building until the 1920s when it moved to its Museum Campus home. Sears Roebuck retail chief Julius Rosenwald then decided that a fortified palace, stripped to its steel frame and rebuilt in limestone, would be the perfect home for a new museum devoted to "industrial enlightenment" and US technological triumphs. The Museum launched around 1933 when Chicago hosted its next World's Fair, Century of Progress Exposition.

TOP 10 FEATURES OF THE 1893 EXPOSITION

1 First ever Ferris Wheel

2 Palace of Fine Arts

3 Midway Plaisance, first separate amusement area at a world's fair

4 Jackson Park, landscaped by designer Frederick Law Olmsted

5 Exotic Dancer "Little Egypt" in the "Streets of Cairo" exhibit

6 The nickname "Windy City" was introduced *(see p113)*

7 A 1,500 lb (680 kg) chocolate Venus de Milo

8 A 70-ft- (21-m-) high tower of light bulbs

9 Floodlights used on buildings for the first time

10 250,000 separate displays on show

The Museum of Science and Industry building started out as the Palace of Fine Arts in 1893.

Present-day Museum of Science and Industry building

TOP 10 ★ Navy Pier

Back in 1995, Chicago's Navy Pier was a drab slab of concrete projecting into Lake Michigan, formerly used as a military and freight terminal. But a huge effort to attract locals and tourists resulted in the installation of a variety of attractions on the waterfront – for kids as well as adults – that draw over nine million people annually, making this Chicago's most visited attraction. The Pier underwent extensive renovations for its 100th anniversary in 2016.

4 Musical Carousel
A quaint merry-go-round of 36 hand-painted horses and chariots next to the Ferris Wheel replicates a similar ride installed on the Pier in the 1920s.

5 Centennial Wheel
It's hard to miss the Pier's 196-ft- (60-m-) high ferris wheel **(right)**, installed in 2016 to replace its smaller predecessor. The slowly revolving ride seats eight in each of its 42 enclosed cars. Daytime rides offer fine lake views, while at night, light shows projected onto the wheel create colorful displays.

1 Wave Swinger
Each of the 48 chain-suspended chairs on this colorful, old-fashioned thrill ride lifts riders 14 ft (5 m) in the air, and spins them until the skyline blurs **(above)**.

2 IMAX® Theatre
The six-story movie theater offers celluloid fare ranging from scientific documentaries to Disney features. Sound and vision headsets aid 3-D movie fun.

3 Polk Bros Park
Navy Pier's front yard is marked by a dramatic fountain with around 250 programmable jets that mimic the movement of water, schools of fish, or flocks of birds. In winter, the park converts into an ice rink.

6 New Food Experience
Replacing run-of-the-mill boardwalk fare, the Pier's newly revamped food court includes several satellites of Chicago-based restaurants such as the two North Side favorites, DMK Burger Bar and Fish Bar.

7 Chicago Children's Museum
Kids love this hands-on museum **(below)** that educates through play. Under-twos get dedicated spaces, including a water room *(see p52)*.

Navy Pier Plan ❸ ❷ ❶ ❻ ❾ ❿

❽ Chicago Shakespeare Theater

This highly respected theater aims to make the Bard accessible to the pleasure-seeking masses visiting Navy Pier. As well as the Shakespearean standards performed here, productions also include the "Short Shakespeare" series for younger audiences.

❾ Amazing Chicago's Funhouse Maze

This mirror-filled, Chicago-themed walking maze leads you on a disorienting, 15-minute journey. Expect spinning lights, startling sound effects, and new perspectives on the city's history and sights. It is an ideal rainy-day attraction.

Richard H. Driehaus ❿ Gallery of Stained Glass

This free-admission gallery features 11 stained-glass windows (right) by decorative arts master Louis Comfort Tiffany. Examples include illuminated windows depicting religious, landscape, and figurative scenes (many saved from Gilded Age mansions).

NEED TO KNOW

MAP M3 ■ 600 E. Grand Ave. ■ CTA Bus: 29, 65, 56, 66, 120, 121 ■ 1-800-595-7437 ■ www.navypier.com

Open summer: 10am–10pm daily (to midnight Fri & Sat); Sep & Oct: 10am–8pm Mon–Sat (to 10pm Fri & Sat); winter: 10am–8pm Mon–Sat (to 10pm Fri & Sat), 10am–7pm Sun

Adm: Free but many attractions charge ■ DA

■ Skip the chain eateries for ribs and live jazz at Joe's Be-Bop Café.

■ In summer the beer garden at the far end of the Pier has stellar city views and free bands.

■ Join a 90-minute lake tour *(see p114)* on a four-masted schooner, or take a ride on a Seadog speedboat.

■ Save money and time spent waiting in line by purchasing a combination ticket for the Musical Carousel, Centennial Wheel, and Wave Swinger.

Orientation
Take public transit, a taxi, or walk to Navy Pier. If driving, you'll find over 1,600 parking spaces right on the Pier. Once there, be sure to stop off at the Guest Services desk, just inside the main entrance, to pick up a schedule for details of the day's events, including performance times and locations for the resident comedy troupe, brass band, and a capella singing group.

Following pages Aerial view across the city to Lake Michigan

🔟 ⭐ John G. Shedd Aquarium

The eponymous John G. Shedd, president of Marshall Field's department store *(see p76)*, donated this Beaux-Arts aquarium to Chicago in 1929. One of the city's top attractions, it houses some 25,500 marine animals representing 2,100 different species that include amphibians, fish, and aquatic mammals. The latter can be seen in the saltwater of the glass-walled Oceanarium, which places an infinity pool in front of Lake Michigan to transporting effect.

1 Caribbean Reef

This vibrant tropical tank **(left)** contains glinting tarpon, bonnethead sharks, fluttering rays, and many other fish. A scuba diver hand-feeds them six times daily, narrating his task via an underwater microphone.

2 Stingray Touch

Dip your hand into the cool, shallow pool filled with stingrays to feel their smooth and muscular wings. The exhibit is the aquarium's first outdoor installation, and therefore closed in winter. Staff manning the pool provide animal interpretation.

3 Animal Enounters

Get up close and personal with Chilean rose tarantulas, African bullfrogs, and red-tailed boas in handler-controlled encounters, held hourly.

4 Waters of the World

Themed tanks hold over 90 re-created aquatic habitats, including Ocean Coasts, Tropical Waters, and Africa, Asia, and Australia. An Australian lungfish, known as "Granddad," has been a resident since 1933.

5 Wild Reef

Gain a daring diver's perspective of whitetip reef, blacktip reef, sand-bar, and zebra sharks **(above)**. The sawfish and fearsome lionfish happily hold their own amid the predator school.

Exterior view of the Shedd

NEED TO KNOW

MAP M6 ■ 1200 S. Lake Shore Dr. ■ "L" station: Roosevelt (Green, Orange, & Red lines) ■ 312-939-2438 ■ www.shedd aquarium.org

Open summer (Memorial Day to Labor Day): 9am–6pm daily (to 10pm Thu Jun–Aug); winter: 9am–5pm Mon–Fri, 9am–6pm Sat & Sun

■ Adm: adults $8; children (3–11) & seniors $6; aquatic show an additional $2 ■ DA

■ Choose one of three dining options at the Shedd: the Soundings serves upscale fare with lake views; the Bubble Net Food Court offers pizzas, sandwiches, and burgers; the Deep Ocean Café offers kid-friendly fare such as hot dogs and mac 'n' cheese.

■ Don't miss the underwater viewing galleries.

■ Check out Jazzin' at the Shedd on Thursdays (5–10pm, adm $20) from June through August.

Aquarium Guide
Consult the day's event schedule printed on the map you're given. Arrive 10–15 minutes early for an Oceanarium Show to get the best seats, and remember that the 20–30-minute Habitat Chats often follow on after the shows.

6 Special Exhibit Gallery

This 3,600-sq-ft (334-sq-m) special exhibit gallery is on the mezzanine level of the Oceanarium and features changing exhibits focused on aquatic animals.

7 4-D Experience

This hi-tech theater experience has "special FX seats" that bombard spectators with bubbles, wind, smells, sounds, and other surprises.

8 Amazon Rising

Demonstrating the huge seasonal tides of the world's longest river, this exhibit presents a year in the life of the Amazon flood plain. Look out for the piranha.

9 Habitat Chats

Oceanarium staffers hold daily discussions about the beluga whales, sea otters, and rockhopper penguins in their charge. Twice daily chats also cover a changing roster of fish at the aquarium.

10 Abbott Oceanarium

Underwater galleries **(left)** afford incredible views of the likes of dolphins and beluga whales swimming through the Oceanarium's vast pools. It is bordered by rocky outcrops and towering pines in a re-creation of the Pacific Northwest coast.

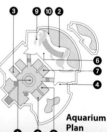

Aquarium Plan

TOP 10 ⭐ Lincoln Park Zoo

Chicago's second most popular attraction after Navy Pier, this menagerie is not only one of the oldest zoos in the country but also one of the last not to charge admission. Established in 1868 with just a pair of swans, the zoo has become an important part of the surrounding North Side community. While small compared to many top US zoos, it is a leading light for ape research, and its park setting, duck ponds, historic café, and landmark red barn endear it to all who visit.

3 Polar Bear Pool

The highlight of this pool is the underwater viewing window (**left**) through which zoo-goers can spy the beautiful sibling bears pawing their way through the water.

4 Regenstein Macaque Forest

A troop of snow monkeys imported from Japan inhabit this forest, which includes treetops for climbing and hot springs.

1 Bird House

Here, a series of habitats showcase their native bird species. And a walk-through tropical aviary allows you to have a close encounter with 20 endangered and exotic species, such as the fairy bluebird, masked lovebird, and green aracari.

2 AT&T Endangered Species Carousel

Ride an artisan-crafted wooden tiger or a bamboo-munching panda on this tent-topped merry-go-round. The carousel is devoted to almost 50 endangered species, many of which are represented in the zoo itself. Admission is charged for this attraction.

Regenstein Small Mammal-Reptile House 5

Replicating the warm climes of South America, Asia, Africa, and Australia, this exhibit introduces the exotic worlds of animals such as snakes (**right**).

6 Regenstein African Journey

Elephants, rhinos (**below**), hippos, and giraffes are among the many animals to roam this expansive exhibit. Totally immerse yourself in the sights and sounds of the varied African landscape around you.

7 Kolver Sea Lion Pool

Despite the name, harbor and gray seals inhabit this pool. Visitors can watch them play at the pool's edge or through an underground viewing window. Try to catch the 2pm training and feeding session.

8 Farm-in-the-Zoo

Keeping city kids in touch with their Midwestern roots, this exhibit offers a daily roster of activities such as goat-milking, cow-feeding, and butter-churning, and the chance to see chicks being born.

Lincoln Park Zoo Plan

9 Kolver Lion House

This 1912 structure stands out not only for its grand architecture but also the grand inhabitants. Many kinds of big cats, including Siberian Tigers **(left)**, prowl – and roar – both inside the hall and in outdoor enclosures.

10 Regenstein Center for African Apes

Simulating the natural habitat of chimps and gorillas **(below)**, this exhibit has huge indoor, tri-level spaces rigged with lifelike trees and vines, as well as an outdoor yard for summer.

NEED TO KNOW

MAP F3 ▪ 2001 N. Clark St. ▪ CTA Bus: 151, 156 ▪ 312-742-2000 ▪ www.lpzoo.org

Open grounds 7am–6pm daily; buildings summer & fall: 10am–5pm daily (summer: to 6:30pm Sat, Sun & hols); winter: 10am–4:30pm daily

Adm: free but $3 charge for AT&T Endangered Species Carousel and Lionel Train Adventure ▪ DA

▪ Check out the Mexican fare year-round at the Park Place Café. In summer, grab a fresh-grilled burger at the historic Café Brauer, which has a beer garden.

▪ Have any animal-related questions? If so, ask staffers at the "Discovery Carts" located all around the zoo.

Visitor Guide

Stop by the Gateway Pavilion (just inside the east gate) when you arrive to pick up a free visitor guide, which has details about feeding times and special events. Staff are on hand here to provide extra information about any new animal arrivals or exhibits. Parking facilities, wheelchairs, lockers, and strollers are also available.

🔟⭐ Magnificent Mile

This glitzy strip of stores and striking buildings runs for, you guessed it, about a mile (1.6 km), along North Michigan Avenue. A sharp developer came up with the "magnificent" moniker in 1947, and it has stuck ever since. Often known as the Mag Mile, it is home to big-guns department stores like Neiman Marcus, as well as high-end boutiques such as Tiffany & Co., and popular chain stores. The strip is at its best around Christmas when twinkling trimmings provide welcome relief from the often gray days.

John Hancock Center ①

When this super-sleek 100-story skyscraper was built in 1970, it was the world's tallest building. Exhilarating views of Chicago and beyond **(right)** are afforded by the 94th-floor observatory and adjoining open-air area, the Skywalk *(see p79)*.

② Hotel InterContinental

Originally built in 1929 as a luxury club for the all-male Shrine association, this amazing hotel *(see p116)* reveals a range of flamboyant architectural styles in its public spaces. You can take a self-guided tour to see the highlights, including the stunning swimming pool **(below)** on the 14th floor.

③ Water Tower Place

Housing a busy shopping mall, this complex is one of the world's tallest reinforced concrete buildings. Its 100-plus shops and venues include a branch of Macy's and a Broadway-style theater.

④ The Drake Hotel

This elegant hotel became an instant glamor hotspot when it opened New Year's Eve in 1920. Marilyn Monroe was among the stars who visited. High tea here is a treat *(see p117)*.

BRIDGE TO SUCCESS

The North Michigan Avenue bascule bridge, built in 1920, was the first of its kind in the world. Instrumental in Chicago's northward expansion, it provides a fitting gateway to the city's main retail artery – the Mag Mile. The southwest tower houses the McCormick Tribune Bridgehouse and River Museum, which details the history of the Chicago River and features displays on the interworkings of this landmark drawbridge.

5 Chicago Water Works and Pumping Station

Dwarfed by the surrounding skyscrapers, these structures are among the few that survived the Great Fire of 1871. The water tower **(left)** contains an art gallery, while the pumping station still functions *(see p80)*.

6 American Girl Place

Eager girls and their moms swarm to this palace of little-girliness *(see p82)*, which stocks all kinds of merchandise from the American Girl doll range. Try the store café or attend the praised musical performance.

7 Wrigley Building

The two towers of the former Wrigley headquarters add to Michigan Avenue's exciting skyline. At night, colored lights illuminate them, as they have done since the building first opened in 1921 *(see p49)*.

Magnificent Mile Map

8 Oak Street

The north end of Mag Mile ends at Oak Street, a lane lined in high-end boutiques. This is one of the most expensive retail spaces in the city *(see p62)*.

9 Museum of Contemporary Art Chicago

Off Michigan Avenue, the strip's cultural gem features compelling temporary exhibits, a sculpture garden, and performing arts *(see p79)*.

10 Tribune Tower

The result of a design competition organized by the *Chicago Tribune* newspaper, this Gothic tower **(left)** is both adored and abhorred by locals. Either way, it's a dramatic Mag Mile landmark *(see p80)*.

NEED TO KNOW

MAP L2–3 ■ Visitor Information: 312-409-5560 ■ "L" Station: Grand/State, Chicago/State
■ www.themagnificentmile.com

Water Tower Place Mall: 835 N. Michigan Ave.; 312-440-3166; open 10am–9pm Mon–Sat & 11am–6pm Sun
■ www.shopwatertower.com

■ Choose from a wide range of high-end, global, fast food at Foodlife food court in Water Tower Place. Food is made fresh daily to eat in or to take out.

■ The Pumping Station houses the main Chicago Visitor Center and a Hot Tix booth (open 10am–6pm Tue–Sat, 11am–4pm Sun) for reduced same-day theater tickets *(see p80)*.

TOP 10 ★ Millennium Park

Designed to celebrate the turn of the 21st century with the reclamation of a former railroad yard in an industrial corner of Grant Park, Millennium Park exceeded its goals in becoming a civic magnet, at least in terms of popularity. Art, architecture, the performing arts, and nature each play a role in the popular park, which hosts summer concerts and special events, and draws visitors year-round to its perennial attractions, led by *Cloud Gate*, its signature sculpture.

Cloud Gate Sculpture **3**

Designed by sculptor Anish Kapoor, the work *Cloud Gate* **(right)** resembles an enlarged, reflective kidney bean, prompting its nickname, "The Bean." A selfie taken here in front of the work reflects the surrounding skyline and is Chicago's signature souvenir.

1 Crown Fountains

Two 50-ft- (15.2-m-) high glass-block towers **(above)** broadcasting the videotaped faces of Chicago residents – keep watching to see if they blink – comprise the Crown Fountains by Spanish artist Jaume Plensa. In summer it's a popular splash park.

4 Lurie Garden

The 15-ft- (4.6-m-) high "shoulder" hedges edging the Lurie Garden pay homage to the "City of Big Shoulders" cited by Carl Sandburg in his poem *Chicago*. They shelter a delicate perennial garden that is spanned by a hardwood footbridge crossing over shallow water.

5 Harris Theater

On the northern fringe of the park, the 1,500-seat state-of-the-art Harris Theater specializes in showcasing music and dance; some 35 Chicago performing arts companies call the Harris home, including Hubbard Street Dance, Music of the Baroque, and Chicago Opera Theater.

Jay Pritzker Pavilion **2**

Designed by the architect Frank Gehry, the centerpiece performing arts venue of the park is framed in flying wings of steel **(right)**. A criss-crossing trellis of speaker-supporting steel pipes extends out over the lawn of this huge concert venue.

6 Ice-Skating Rink

The Millennium Park ice-skating rink (left), generally open between December and March (weather permitting), is free, which perhaps accounts for the throngs of skaters here, eager to glide under the "The Bean."

7 Park Grill

The only restaurant in Millennium Park, Park Grill doesn't rest on its location. The quality meals provide the perfect accompaniment to the views of the city skyline, from casual burgers to more upscale fare. In warm weather, tables sprawl out onto the terrace, which serves as the skating rink in winter.

8 Millennium Monument

Anchoring the northwest corner of the park at tree-lined Wrigley Square, a semi-circular peristyle, or row of 40-ft (12-m) Doric-style columns, recall the original classical monument that stood here in the first half of the 20th century. It's now an attractive backdrop to the modern city.

Millennium Park Map

9 Nichols Bridgeway

Architect Renzo Piano, who designed the Modern Wing addition to the Art Institute of Chicago, also worked on this bridge, which gradually rises from the park to the second story of the museum across the street.

10 BP Bridge

The bridge (below) connecting Millennium Park to neighboring Maggie Daley Park (see p52) was designed by Frank Gehry. The steel-clad winding structure offers views of Lake Michigan, the skyline, and Millennium Park, and takes an intentionally indirect route.

NEED TO KNOW

MAP L4 ▪ 201 E. Randolph St. ▪ 312-742-1168 ▪ www.millenniumpark.org

Park: 6am–11pm daily

Welcome Center: 312-742-2963; open May–Sep: 9am–7pm; Oct–Apr: 10am–4pm

▪ There are free 45-minute guided tours twice daily in May–Oct. Ask at the Welcome Center for details.

TOP 10 ⭐ Frank Lloyd Wright's Oak Park

This suburb, 7 miles (11 km) west of downtown Chicago, contains the world's largest collection of Frank Lloyd Wright-designed buildings. It was here that Wright developed his Prairie style (inspired by the flat lines of the Midwestern plains). His work was initially considered radical compared to the typical styles of the day. Walking through Oak Park's quaint, tree-lined streets, it's evident that Wright's architecture stands out from the norm – but in all the right ways.

FRANK LLOYD WRIGHT

After moving to Oak Park in 1889, Wright (1867–1959) appeared to lead the perfect suburban life. But in the early 20th century he caused scandal by gallivanting with married women and wearing flamboyant clothes. During the Depression, he changed into a respected social visionary, and later redefined himself as a quick-witted sage. Ultimately, he established himself as the first celebrity architect.

Unity Temple 2

This compact church (1908) superbly demonstrates Wright's use of poured concrete for both structural and decorative purposes (right).

1 Beachy House

This impressive 1906 home contradicts many of Wright's trademarks. Instead of just stucco and wood or brick and concrete, he used them all: it also has a seven-gabled, rather than a hipped, roof.

3 Frank Lloyd Wright Home and Studio

Built when the famous architect moved to Oak Park (1889), this house (above) is where Wright designed over 150 structures. The children's playroom is luminous with signature art-glass windows.

5 Charles Matthews House

Chicago architects Thomas Eddy Tallmadge and Vernon S. Watson designed this elegant 1909 Prairie-style residence for a wealthy pharmacist. Among the notable interior details are Prairie-inspired light fixtures and folding art-glass doors.

4 Pleasant Home

This 30-room Prairie-style 1897 home (left) built by George Maher, was Oak Park's first to have electricity. The 30-room architectural gem holds a small history museum, with exhibits relating to Tarzan creator and former local resident, Edgar Rice Burroughs.

6 Edwin Cheney House

This home sparked a tragic love affair between Wright and Mamah Cheney, leading him to abandon his family and practice. Mamah and her children were murdered at Wright's home by an insane servant in 1914.

7 The Bootleg Houses

Wright lost his job over these three private commissions, built while he was employed by Louis H. Sullivan (see p43). Though Queen Anne-like in style, they hint at the design elements that were to be his hallmarks.

8 Arthur Heurtley House

Wright's beautiful 1902 house (above) is absolute Prairie, with its low, wide chimney, and band of art-glass windows that makes the overhanging roof appear to float.

9 Nathan Moore House

Out of financial desperation, Wright built this charming Tudor-style home for his neighbor. After a fire destroyed the top floors in 1922, Wright's modifications echoed his West Coast concrete block houses.

NEED TO KNOW

MAP A4 ■ "L" Station: Oak Park

Frank Lloyd Wright Home & Studio: 951 Chicago Ave.; 312-994-4000; www.gowright.org; open 10am–5pm daily

Unity Temple: 875 West Lake St.

Pleasant Home: 217 South Home Ave.

Arthur Heurtley House: 318 Forest Ave.

The Bootleg Houses: 1019/1027/1031 Chicago Ave.

Charles Matthews House: 432 North Kenilworth Ave.

Edwin Cheney House: 520 North East Ave.

Beachy House: 238 Forest Ave.

Nathan Moore House: 333 Forest Ave.

Harry Adams House: 710 Augusta Blvd.

■ The Oak Park Visitors' Center (1010 Lake St.) sells maps, books, and tour tickets.

Oak Park Street Map

10 Harry Adams House

This striking 1913 home marks the last of Wright's Oak Park houses and features several of the elements that made him famous, such as exquisite stained glass, and a low overhanging roof.

The Top 10 of Everything

Stunning spiral staircase, The Rookery, S. LaSalle St.

⓾ Moments in Chicago History

The Great Chicago Fire of 1871

① 1871: Great Chicago Fire

Over 250 people died and 17,000 buildings were destroyed in this fire, allegedly started by a cow kicking over a lantern. Just a few buildings survived, including the Historic Water Tower and Pumping Station *(see p80)*.

② 1885: First Skyscraper

Though just a measly – by today's standards – nine stories, the Home Insurance Building (now demolished) was the tallest of its time. William Le Baron Jenney achieved this architectural feat by designing the first weight-bearing steel frame. From then on, the only way to go was up.

③ 1886: Haymarket Riot

Wealthy industrialists funded amazing Chicago arts institutions, but their workers toiled long hours in abominable conditions. In May 1886, a labor protest ended in an explosion at Haymarket Square that killed eight policemen and two bystanders. Eight anarchists were convicted of murder, though three were later pardoned for lack of evidence.

④ 1892: First Elevated Train

The first train traveled just 3.6 miles (5.8 km) along tracks built above city-owned alleys (avoiding the need to negotiate with private property owners). By 1893, the line was extended to Jackson Park *(see p46)* to transport visitors to the World's Columbian Exposition *(see p23)*.

⑤ 1900: Reversal of the Chicago River

With sewage flowing downriver to Lake Michigan, the source of the city's drinking water, thousands of Chicagoans were dying from the contamination. To solve the problem, engineers created a canal that forced the river to flow away from the lake: an extraordinary feat of engineering.

⑥ 1919: Chicago Black Sox Scandal

The Chicago White Sox was a winning baseball team but poorly paid, so players sometimes fixed games, pocketing money from gamblers. After a group of players conspired to lose the 1919 World Series, eight of them were indicted, acquitted for insufficient evidence, but banned for life from baseball – and nicknamed the "Black Sox."

Chicago White Sox baseball team

⑦ 1929: Valentine's Day Massacre

This brutal murder of seven of Al Capone's rival gangsters is one of US history's most notorious massacres. Capone set up a sting that sent George "Bugs" Moran's main men to a nearby garage. There, Capone's henchmen, dressed as police officers, lined them up and riddled them with bullets. Seven bushes now mark the spot (at Clark Street and Dickens Avenue).

Enrico Fermi

8 1942: First Atom Split

Under the football stands on the campus of the University of Chicago, Enrico Fermi made history. He supervised the creation of a primitive nuclear reactor and took the first major step in understanding how to build an atomic bomb.

9 1955: First McDonald's Franchise Opens

Ray Kroc, a milkshake mixer salesman, changed diets worldwide by convincing Dick and Mac McDonald to franchise their San Bernardino, California burger stand. The original restaurant in Des Plaines – 15 miles (24 km) west of Chicago – is now a museum.

10 2008: Barack Obama Elected President

Chicago had elected its first black mayor, Harold Washington, in 1983, but a new national barrier was vaulted with the 2008 election of Illinois senator Barack Obama as president. Thousands of jubilant voters gathered at the public rally in Grant Park on election night to celebrate the historic event.

Barack Obama wins the 2008 election

TOP 10 CHICAGO RESIDENTS

Benny Goodman

1 Jean Baptiste Point du Sable
Chicago's first non-native settler was an African-American trader who set up camp around 1779.

2 Jane Addams
This social activist (1860–1935) founded Hull House social center *(see p97)* and won a Nobel Peace Prize.

3 Carl Sandburg
One of Chicago's nicknames, "City of the big shoulders," was penned by this author/poet (1878–1967).

4 Al Capone
America's best-known mobster (1899–1947) was Chicago's "Public Enemy Number One" until jailed in 1931 for tax evasion.

5 Ernest Hemingway
Born in Oak Park, this hard-living author (1899–1961) left the suburb of "wide lawns and narrow minds" at age 19.

6 Benny Goodman
Born to Russian-Jewish immigrants, jazz great Goodman (1909–1986) earned the title "King of Swing."

7 Hugh Hefner
Hefner (1926–) is the notorious lothario and founder of *Playboy*, whose first issue sold over 50,000 copies.

8 Curtis Mayfield
Soul musician and social activist (1942–99), Mayfield had his first hit *For Your Precious Love* at the age of 16.

9 Oprah Winfrey
TV's talk-show darling (1954–) filmed in Chicago from 1984 to 2011 and has become an honorary native of the city.

10 Barack Obama
The former US President (1961–) taught at the Chicago Law School from 1992 to 2004. His residential home is in the Kenwood neighborhood.

🔟 Skyscrapers

1 The Rookery
One of the earliest remaining skyscrapers, this 1888 landmark (see p72) combines traditional wall-bearing and newer steel-frame construction. The latter made it possible for its architects, Burnham and Root, to design an open interior, with offices set around a central light well.

The 100-story John Hancock Center

2 John Hancock Center
The tapering, 100-story John Hancock Center is somewhat overshadowed by the higher Willis Tower but is arguably more distinctive. Designed by Skidmore, Owings & Merrill, who also did the Willis, it features its own observatory on the 94th floor (see p79).

3 Auditorium Theatre
MAP L5 ▪ 50 E. Congress Pkwy.
▪ For tours call 312-341-2389
Built by Adler and Sullivan in 1889, the ornate Auditorium also originally contained a hotel and office building and had one of the first public air-conditioning systems. The revamped 4,000-seat theater boasts near-perfect acoustics.

4 Reliance Building
The steel skeleton on this 1895-built skyscraper allowed it to be wrapped in glass. It offers a fine example of the Chicago window, characterized by a bay window placed between two narrow, double-hung windows. Occupied by the Hotel Burnham (see p117) the inside has replicas of original features (see p74).

5 860–80 N. Lake Shore Drive
MAP L2
You might think these two high-rise apartment buildings (1949–51) look like the others along this classy strip. Actually, the others look like these. Architect Mies van der Rohe perfected the "less is more" approach, which so many other architects went on to copy.

6 Willis Tower
This soaring tower, built in 1973 for retailer Sears Roebuck and Co. (who have since moved out), can be seen from almost anywhere in the city. Its Skydeck affords sensational views (see pp12–13).

7 Marina City
With its twin cylindrical structures (1959–64) on the Chicago River, Marina City (see p12) is a "city within a city," containing offices, residences, a theater, and more. The apartments afford spectacular views, but their shape creates some interior decorating challenges.

Marina City

The innovative exterior of Aqua Tower

⑧ Aqua Tower
MAP L3 ▪ 225 N. Columbus Dr.
The exterior of the 84-story Aqua Tower appears to undulate due to the varying elevations of the skyscraper's balconies. Architect Jeanne Gang cites the striated limestone outcroppings that are common along Great Lakes shorelines.

⑨ Monadnock Building
Constructed in two stages, this Loop edifice represents the evolution of skyscraper architecture. The northern half was built in 1891 using solely wall-bearing construction, while the southern half was built two years later and incorporated the then-emerging steel-frame technology still used today (see p74).

⑩ Tribune Tower
Despite the cathedral-like buttresses atop the Tribune Tower, headquarters of the Chicago Tribune, this Neo-Gothic building was only erected in 1925. Its facade contains stones from 120 global landmarks, including China's Great Wall (see p80).

TOP 10 CHICAGO ARCHITECTS

1 William Le Baron Jenney
The "father of the skyscraper" (1832–1907) who designed the first all-metal-framed structure, the Home Insurance Building, in 1885 (see p40).

2 Daniel Burnham
Visionary city planner and architect, Burnham (1846–1912) was the man behind the White City (see p23).

3 William Holabird & Martin Roche
This influential team (Holabird 1854–1923; Roche 1853–1927) developed early Chicago-style skyscrapers including the Marquette Building (see p74).

4 Louis H. Sullivan
The creator (1856–1924) of the "form follows function" doctrine designed according to a building's intended use.

5 Frank Lloyd Wright
Inspired by the wide open spaces of the Midwest, Wright (see pp36–7) was the originator of the Prairie style.

6 George Maher
A Prairie School architect (1864–1926) who favored Arts and Crafts motifs.

7 Walter Burley Griffin
Another Prairie-style architect (1876–1937) with a namesake historic district on Chicago's South Side.

8 Ludwig Mies van der Rohe
This minimalist architect (1886–1969) was the creator of the modern glass-and-steel box.

9 Bertrand Goldberg
Goldberg (1913–1997) designed Marina City, which is typical of his curvilinear concrete shapes.

10 Jeanne Gang
Designer of the award-winning Aqua Tower, Gang (1964–) is a contemporary innovator among skyscraper designers.

Frank Lloyd Wright

🔟 Niche Museums

immigrants, this tiny museum's permanent collection of personal items brought over by early settlers is supplemented by temporary exhibitions on Swedish culture. An interactive children's museum brings the immigrant journey to life.

3 Hellenic Museum and Cultural Center

MAP H5 ■ 333 S. Halsted St. ■ 11am–5pm Tue–Fri (to 8pm Thu), 11am–5pm Sat & Sun ■ Adm: $10; students and seniors $8; members and under-3s free ■ www. hellenicmuseum.org

Located in the city's Greektown, this museum is dedicated to celebrating Hellenic culture and the Greek immigrant experience in America.

4 National Museum of Mexican Art

MAP B5 ■ 1852 W. 19th St. ■ 10am–5pm Tue–Sun ■ DA ■ www. nationalmuseumofmexicanart.org

The largest Latino museum in the US explores the culture *sin fronteras* (without boundaries), showing works from Mexican and Mexican-American communities. Pre-Columbian ceramics, Day of the dead candelabras, and prints by Diego Rivera are highlights of the collection.

1 Spertus Museum

MAP L6 ■ 610 S. Michigan Ave. ■ 10am–5pm Sun, Mon & Wed (to 6pm Thu & 3pm Fri) ■ DA ■ www.spertus.edu

From cartoons to ancient Torah scrolls, this museum offers a lively, multifaceted retelling of Jewish history and culture. The museum's Zell Holocaust Memorial was the first such permanent installation in the US.

National Museum of Mexican Art

2 Swedish American Museum

MAP B3 ■ 5211 N. Clark St. ■ 10am–4pm Tue–Fri, 11am–4pm Sat & Sun ■ Adm: $4; children, seniors, students $3 ■ DA ■ www.swedishamericanmuseum.org

Located in Andersonville, the historic neighborhood of Scandinavian

5 DuSable Museum of African American History

Named for Jean Baptiste Point du Sable, Chicago's first settler (who was of African descent), this enthralling museum chronicles

Mosaic at the DuSable Museum of African American History

the African-American experience. There is a powerful exhibit on slavery, complete with shackles, while displays cover topics such as African hair art and the *Kwanzaa* holiday celebration *(see p101)*.

6 Ukrainian Institute of Modern Art

MAP B4 ■ 2320 W. Chicago Ave. ■ noon–4pm Wed–Sun ■ www.uima-chicago.org

This tiny institute in the colorful Ukrainian Village neighborhood hosts rotating cultural programs, exhibitions, literary events, film screenings, and concerts. The permanent collection includes works by Chicago artists, as well as by painters and sculptors of Ukrainian descent.

Sculpture in Ukrainian Institute of Modern Art

7 International Museum of Surgical Science

MAP F4 ■ 1524 N. Lake Shore Dr. ■ 10am–4pm Tue–Fri, 10am–5pm Sat & Sun ■ Adm (free Tue): $15; students and seniors $10, children (4–13) $7, members and under-3s free ■ DA

Medicine meets the macabre at this museum, which displays historic instruments that span 4,000 years of surgery. Murals and sculptures pay tribute to the profession. Stronger stomachs may appreciate the ancient Peruvian skulls showing evidence of early surgical attempts.

8 Mary & Leigh Block Museum of Art

MAP B2 ■ 40 Arts Circle Dr., Evanston ■ 10am–5pm Tue, 10am–8pm Wed–Fri, 10am–5pm Sat & Sun

This collection of paintings, drawings, and sculpture is housed in a striking glass and limestone building designed by local architect Dirk Lohan. The museum offers rotating exhibitions, as well as numerous timely lectures and workshops.

9 Oriental Institute

In the heart of the University of Chicago campus, this museum showcases the work of University of Chicago researchers. It houses objects found in excavations in Egypt, Nubia, Persia, Mesopotamia, Syria, Anatolia, and ancient Megiddo. There are also temporary exhibitions *(see p102)*.

10 Jane Addams Hull House

Nobel Peace Prize-winning social reformer Jane Addams offered a brighter future to Chicago's immigrant population from these two Victorian houses. In addition to her original art and furniture, Hull House stages temporary exhibits relating to the social settlement that brought day care, counseling, and education to the working class *(see p97)*.

🔟 Parks and Beaches

1 Millennium and Grant Parks

As well as a center for world-class art, music, architecture, and landscape design, Millennium Park offers winter ice-skating, interactive public art, alfresco dining, and free classical music concerts and film screenings. Together with the adjoining 19th-century Grant Park, which hosts many festivals (see pp66–7), it constitutes one of the finest, user-friendly green spaces in Chicago (see p72).

2 North Avenue Beach

Chicago's most popular beach attracts a broad range of urban dwellers. Its lively ocean-liner-shaped bathhouse (including umbrella rentals, shower rooms, snack vendors, and a rooftop restaurant) makes it family friendly. Beach volleyball courts and a seasonal outdoor gym are a big draw (see p89).

Volleyball at North Avenue Beach

3 Oak Street Beach
MAP L1

At the foot of the chic Gold Coast shopping lane, this beach reflects its environs. Though just next to North Avenue Beach, you won't see many children here. Oak Street is usually filled with toned bodies and tiny bikinis. The crescent-shaped strand is the closest beach to the Magnificent Mile (see pp32–3) and makes a great place to stop and dip your toes after some serious shopping.

Kid's playground, Maggie Daley Park

4 Maggie Daley Park

Maggie Daley Park marks the northeastern boundary of Grant Park. Named for the former first lady of Chicago, the park offers a range of diversions, including a seasonal ice-skating ribbon, climbing walls, and an elaborate playground for children. There are also tennis courts, picnic tables, and a garden dedicated to cancer survivors (see p52).

5 Jackson Park
MAP F6

Laid out by the famed landscape designer Frederick Law Olmsted for the 1893 World's Columbian Exposition, Jackson Park, along with its Museum of Science and Industry (see pp20–21), is among the few developments still remaining from that World's Fair. The South Side park includes a Japanese garden with waterfalls, colorful lanterns, and a bird sanctuary on an island in a peaceful lagoon.

6 Montrose Beach
MAP C3

Chicago's largest public beach is popular with families. Great for swimming, it has a changing house and shower facilities. Other activities include volleyball, sailboat and jet ski rentals, and a large number of trails for running and biking. The vast playing fields wedged between the sand and Lake Shore Drive are the domain of Hispanic soccer clubs: on weekends their numbers draw Latin food and balloon vendors. Kayak rentals launch here in summer.

7 Washington Square
MAP K2

Located opposite the historic Newberry Library, Washington Square is a prime plot of Gold Coast for resting tired feet and gazing at the handsome 1892 building. The park's ample benches tend to draw bookish sorts and picnicking office workers at lunchtime.

8 Lincoln Park
MAP F3

The greenway Lincoln Park stretches from North Avenue up to Hollywood Avenue, a recreational apron between lakefront and housing. In Chicago's infancy, the southern portion of the park was a cemetery for Civil War dead, which were later exhumed and interred elsewhere to make way for the park. Now Lincoln Park is the North Side's counterpart to Grant Park. Popular attractions such as Lincoln Park Zoo *(see pp30–31)*, the Lincoln Park Conservatory *(see p88)*, and Peggy Notebaert Nature Museum *(see p87)* supplement the beaches, harbors, playing fields, and bike paths.

South Pond Pavilion, Lincoln Park

9 Northerly Island
MAP M6

A peninsula jutting out in Lake Michigan south of the Alder Planetarium, Northerly Island is home to prairie plants, walking trails, and fountains. In summer it hosts concerts and special events at an outdoor stage that can accommodate 30,000 people on its lawn.

10 Ping Tom Memorial Park
MAP K6

Named in honor of a prominent Chinese businessman and civic leader, this rolling green space in Chinatown features Chinese design elements and public access to the river. A boat house offers kayak rentals in summer, and the field house hosts an indoor gym and swimming pool.

🔟 Film Locations

The Field Museum in *The Relic*

3 Field Museum
Scare-fest *The Relic* (1997) starred Penelope Ann Miller and Tom Sizemore as researchers trying to stop a murderous monster before it killed again. Many interior scenes were shot on replica sets but were near-perfect matches to the real museum (see pp18–19).

1 Michigan Avenue Bridge
In *Chain Reaction* (1996), Keanu Reeves is a science student at the University of Chicago (see p101) who is framed for murder. In a nail-biting chase scene, he tries to escape by running up the Michigan Avenue Bridge (see p32) as it's raised.

4 Wrigley Field
The 1914-vintage Wrigley Field (see p87), home to the Chicago Cubs, has starred in numerous baseball movies, including *The Natural*, *Rookie of the Year*, and *A League of Their Own*. It also has a cameo in *The Blues Brothers* and *Ferris Bueller's Day Off*.

5 Drake Hotel
In feel-good film *Hero* (1992), John Bubber (Andy Garcia) dupes the public into thinking he's a hero. Feeling guilty, he resolves to jump off a window ledge at The Drake (see p117). Reality interrupted the filming when guests arrived for a party at the hotel. Director Stephen Frears protested and almost got arrested.

Michigan Avenue Bridge, featured in *Chain Reaction*

2 Daley Center and Plaza
Daley Plaza (see p75) was the setting for a chase scene in cult movie classic *The Blues Brothers* (1980). Stars John Belushi and Dan Aykroyd, playing ex-criminal brothers, dramatically crash their car through the center's plate-glass windows, specially installed for the filming.

A scene from *Hero* in the Drake Hotel

6 Palmer House Hilton

Wrongly accused and convicted of murder, Dr. Richard Kimble (Harrison Ford) dodges the authorities led by Tommy Lee Jones to prove his innocence in *The Fugitive* (1993). He winds up in a pulse-pounding chase through this grand hotel *(see p117)* onto its roof, down its elevator shaft, and into the hotel's laundry room.

7 Randolph "L" Station
MAP L4

The "L" tracks are an apt symbol of hard-working Chicago, and they feature significantly in the romantic comedy *While You Were Sleeping* (1995). Sandra Bullock plays an "L" station clerk who falls in love with a handsome commuter. He tumbles off the platform, Bullock saves his life, and comedy and romance ensue.

8 Wrigley Building

In *Road to Perdition* (2002) Tom Hanks is Michael Sullivan, an Irish gangster living in 1930s Chicago. After his wife and young son are murdered, he flees town with his older son. In seeking a safe refuge, they enter a hotel, the exterior of which is the beautiful Wrigley Building *(see p33)*. However, the interior scenes were actually filmed at the Palmer House Hilton.

9 The Art Institute of Chicago

The high-school comedy *Ferris Bueller's Day Off* (1986) stars Matthew Broderick, who skips school and takes his girlfriend (Mia Sara) and best friend (Alan Ruck) on an action-packed day. At the Art Institute, Broderick and Sara kiss in front of a window designed by Chagall, while Ruck stares intensely at *A Sunday on La Grande Jatte –1884 (see pp14–15)*.

Ferris at The Art Institute of Chicago

10 Union Station
MAP J4 ■ 210 S. Canal St.

Elliott Ness (Kevin Costner) brings down Chicago gangster Al Capone (Robert DeNiro) in the true story *The Untouchables* (1987). In one unforgettable scene, a shoot-out on a Union Station staircase causes a mother to lose her grip on her baby carriage, which bounces in slow motion down the stairs, saved at the last moment by Ness's partner.

Union Station staircase sets the scene for *The Untouchables*

⟪TOP 10⟫ Off the Beaten Path

① University of Chicago
Funded by oil magnate John D. Rockefeller (who deemed it his best ever investment), this forward-thinking institution opened in 1892 (see p101). The university campus is home to an attractive Neo-Gothic quad, the Oriental Institute (see p102), the Smart Museum of Art, the soaring Rockefeller Memorial Chapel, and Robie House (see p102).

② Chicago Botanic Garden
MAP A1 ▪ 1000 Lake Cook Rd., Glencoe ▪ Metra station: Braeside ▪ 1-847-835-5440 ▪ Open 8am–sunset daily ▪ Adm ▪ DA ▪ www.chicago-botanic.org

North of Chicago are these natural and beautifully landscaped gardens. The most popular are the Rose Garden, the Japanese Garden, and the charming English Walled Garden.

③ Evanston
MAP B2 ▪ "L" station: Davis ▪ Visitors' Bureau: 1-847-448-4311

This suburb brims with restaurants, galleries, and shops. Northwestern University's Mary & Leigh Block Museum of Art (see p45) and Grosse Point Lighthouse are worth a visit.

The stunning Baha'i Temple

④ Baha'i Temple
MAP A1 ▪ 100 Linden Ave., Wilmette ▪ "L" station: Linden Ave. ▪ Visitors' Center open mid-May–mid-Sep 10am–8pm daily (to 5pm rest of the year); temple open 6am–10pm daily ▪ 1-847-853-2300 ▪ DA

This exquisite white structure is one of only eight temples of the Baha'i faith worldwide. Its nine doors symbolize how people can come to God from any direction. At night, spotlights enhance its ethereal beauty and intricate design.

⑤ Brookfield Zoo
MAP A6 ▪ 8400 W. 31st St., Brookfield ▪ Metra station: Hollywood ▪ CTA Bus: 331 ▪ 1-708-688-8000 ▪ Open 10am–5pm daily ▪ Adm (under-2s free) ▪ DA

Over 5,900 animals live together in themed, naturalistic environments at this popular zoo. Zones include Tropic World, where thunderstorms occur regularly (you stay dry) and Habitat Africa!, whose Forest exhibit has shy okapi and a re-created African village. In Be A Bird House, see what kind of bird you'd be on a machine that measures your flapping ability.

6 Bronzeville

MAP C5 ■ "L" station:
35th-Bronzeville-IIT (Green line)

A bronze memorial at Martin Luther King, Jr. Drive and 35th Street honors the journey many African-Americans made to this neighborhood as they fled the oppression of the South in the early 20th century. Nearby, sidewalk plaques celebrate local luminaries. Bronzeville is Chicago's answer to Harlem and offers jazz and blues in its clubs, graceful mansions aplenty, and lots of fine soul food.

7 Hemingway Birthplace

MAP A5 ■ "L" station: Oak Park
■ 1-708-524-5383 ■ Open 1–5pm
Sun–Fri, 10am–5pm Sat ■ Adm
■ www.ehfop.org

Oak Park (see pp36–7) is well known as the first professional home of architect Frank Lloyd Wright, and for the concentration of Wright-designed buildings he left behind. But Oak Park was also home to a young Ernest Hemingway; the author's birthplace is open for tours.

8 Illinois Institute of Technology (IIT)

MAP C5 ■ 3300 S. Federal St. ■ "L" station: 35th-Bronzeville-IIT (Green line) ■ 312-567-3000 ■ Tours: www.miessociety.org/home/tours ■ DA

In 1940, Ludwig Mies van der Rohe planned the campus of this new university. He also designed around 20 of the buildings, which demonstrate his design philosophies. On arrival, stop by the on-campus visitor center for information and docent- or iPod-guided tours.

Illinois Institute of Technology

9 Garfield Park Conservatory

MAP B5 ■ 300 N. Central Park Ave.
■ "L" station: Conservatory-Central Park Dr. (Green line) ■ 312-746-5100
■ Open 9am–5pm daily (to 8pm Wed)
■ DA ■ www.garfield-conservatory.org

Beneath glass-domed roofs, flora from around the world thrives in spacious greenhouses. Information panels give the lowdown as you stroll through six indoor areas that include a Children's Garden and the Sweet House (containing plants such as cacao and sugar cane). Two grand exhibition halls host special events.

Garfield Park Conservatory

10 Pullman National Monument

MAP B6 ■ Metra Station: Pullman/
111th St. ■ Visitors' Center: 11141 S. Cottage Grove Ave., open 11am–3pm Tue–Sun ■ 1-773-785-8901 ■ DA

Named a National Monument in 2015, this industrial town was conceived in the 1880s by railroad magnate George Pullman for his workers. The planned utopia had apartments, shops, a hospital, and a hotel, but failed after a strike in 1894, when a decrease in wages made rents unaffordable.

🔟 Kids' Chicago

① Emerald City Theatre Company

MAP D2 ▪ 2936 N. Southport Ave.
▪ 1-773-529-2690 ▪ Open Oct–May
▪ www.emeraldcitytheatre.com
▪ Adm

In Chicago there's a theater company for every demographic and Emerald City is its troupe devoted to young audiences. Expect lively productions such as *Where the Wild Things Are* as well as holiday-season shows in weekend-only midday matinees at Lincoln Park's Apollo Theater.

② Maggie Daley Park

This 20-acre park *(see p75)*, tucked between Millennium Park and Lake Shore Drive, is a superb recreation area. The vast Play Garden for kids aged 12 and under has a pirate ship, swinging bridge, rope ladder, and Enchanted Forest with meandering paths and a rolling Wave Lawn. A seasonal ice ribbon makes a curvy path around the park's two rock climbing walls, which include routes for beginners (children must be able to wear the harnesses provided, which generally do not fit children under the age of 4), as well as for advanced climbers.

Display in Chicago Children's Museum

③ Chicago Children's Museum

MAP M3 ▪ 700 E. Grand Ave. ▪ 312-527-1000 ▪ Opening times vary ▪ Adm
▪ www.chicagochildrensmuseum.org

The engrossing, imaginative exhibits here emphasize doing – be it digging up a dinosaur bone or designing a water channel. A central, three-story rope tunnel immediately snares the attention of older visitors, though there are age-appropriate attractions for infants to pre-teens. If this place can't exhaust the younger set's energies, nowhere can.

④ Wrigley Field

A baseball-lover's park, Wrigley is a small and intimate stadium that's far less intimidating for children than many larger stadia *(see p87)*. A ticket to anywhere in the grandstand allows you to walk around and get to the rooftop terrace: the outfield stands can get rowdy, but a neighboring family section bans the beer that fuels the "bleacher bums."

⑤ Elevated Trains

Chicago's elevated trains (the "L") provide an inexpensive roofline tour of the city. The Brown Line in particular warrants a ride from Chicago Station over the Chicago River and around the Loop, threading between the massive buildings of the financial district *(see p108)*.

6 Chicago River Boat Tours

Even the smallest visitors will love a boat ride on the Chicago River, floating among the towering skyscrapers and listening to stories of the city and of how the river's flow was reversed to spare Lake Michigan its pollution. Wendella and Shoreline Sightseeing *(see p115)* both embark from Michigan Avenue, and offer family-friendly narration, from spring through to fall.

7 Lincoln Park Zoo

Free admission encourages repeat visits to the Lincoln Park Zoo *(see pp30–31)*. Many of the exhibits, including the working Farm in the Zoo and the Children's Zoo, allow kids to pet the animals. In summer, a motorized "train" makes a scenic loop around the park, while on the pond, swan-shaped paddleboats float among the ducks.

8 John G. Shedd Aquarium

Upon arrival, head straight for the Abbott Oceanarium to see the beluga whales and dolphins. Wild Reef re-creates a coral reef and houses sharks and other large predators. In the Polar Play Zone, kids can don a penguin suit and waddle in the Icy South play area or explore Arctic waters in the Icy North in a kids' size submarine. Children will also enjoy the special effects 4-D theater *(see pp28–9)*.

Dolphins at play, Shedd Aquarium

9 Museum of Science and Industry

Though this museum dazzles kids and adults alike with its submarine ship and replica coal mine, it's The Idea Factory that's designed just for juniors. With the pulling of gears and shifting of knobs, kids experiment through play with balance, construction, magnetism, and more. A current-fed waterway encourages boat building *(see pp20–23)*.

Maze, Museum of Science and Industry

10 Navy Pier

Kids make a beeline for Navy Pier's traditional carnival rides including a 196-ft- (60-m-) high ferris wheel and musical carousel. The ships that line the docks, from sleek, tall-masted schooners to powerful motorboats, will also grab their attention. All the restaurants here are family friendly *(see pp24–5)*.

🔟 Performing Arts

Inside the Civic Opera House

the University of Chicago in 1955. The Court still mounts many classics, but it varies its seasons with musicals like *Guys and Dolls* and literary adaptations such as James Joyce's *The Dead*.

1 Lyric Opera of Chicago

Established in 1954, the Lyric Opera is among the leading companies in the US, drawing top singers and directors. From September through May it offers a mix of classical operas, modern premieres, and popular musicals. Most are performed at the ornate Art Deco Civic Opera House, with its gleaming marble floors and crystal chandeliers *(see p75)*.

2 Court Theatre
MAP E5 ▪ 5535 S. Ellis Ave.
▪ www.courttheatre.org
This theater traces its roots to three Molière productions performed at

3 Chicago Symphony Orchestra

Conductor Riccardo Muti presides over the esteemed Chicago Symphony Orchestra and cellist Yo-Yo Ma is its creative consultant. The orchestra performs classical and contemporary pieces, with pop culture programs such as film scores thrown in. The orchestra's main home is the magnificent Symphony Center *(see p75)*, but in summer they play at the outdoor suburban venue Ravinia.

4 Steppenwolf Theatre Co.

Founded in 1974 in a church basement, Steppenwolf has gained acclaim based on the fame of its ensemble, which includes actors John Malkovich and Gary Sinise. Though the company has moved to a specially built theater in Lincoln Park, it is still distinguished by raw emotion and edgy productions, and has received many notable accolades, including 12 Tony® Awards *(see p88)*.

A performance at the Court Theatre

5 Goodman Theatre
MAP K3 ■ 170 N. Dearborn St.
■ www.goodmantheatre.org
One of Chicago's leading theater companies, the Goodman frequently spins off productions to Broadway in New York and has earned a Tony® Award. Noted productions include dramas by Eugene O'Neill and August Wilson and an annual version of Charles Dickens' *A Christmas Carol*.

6 Second City
MAP K2 ■ 1616 N. Wells St. ■ www. secondcity.com
Since 1959, Chicago's famed Second City comedy troupe has launched such comic lights as Tina Fey, Amy Poehler, and Bill Murray. Reservations are a must.

Facade detail, Second City

7 Chicago Shakespeare Theater
MAP M3 ■ 800 E. Grand Ave.
■ www.chicagoshakes.com
This Navy Pier venue presents a dynamic space for Shakespeare's repertory. The 510-seat courtyard design is inspired by the original layout in traditional playhouses of the Bard's day. Visiting non-Shakespeare productions take over after the company's September-to-April season.

8 Old Town School of Folk Music
MAP E3 ■ 4544 N. Lincoln Ave.
■ www.oldtownschool.org
Since the 1950s the Old Town School has brought world and homegrown folk music performers to Chicago. Its new home in Lincoln Square opened in 1998 with a concert by Joni Mitchell, though you're more likely to catch a women's ensemble from Mali and contemporary folkies.

9 Lookingglass Theatre
MAP L2 ■ 821 N. Michigan Ave.
■ www.lookingglasstheatre.org
In 1988, eight Northwestern University students founded Lookingglass, a bold company incorporating dance, circus arts, and live music in its original theatrical productions. Celebrity membership (including *Friends* actor David Schwimmer) and Broadway-bound shows have furthered this company's stardom.

10 House Theatre
MAP B4 ■ 1543 W. Division St.
■ www.thehousetheatre.com
Though it has moved out of storefronts and into the spacious Chopin Theater, this small troop epitomizes the creativity of Chicago theater. The group frequently writes its own works, which often cover epic themes and are popular with families.

🔟 Blues and Jazz Joints

Entrance to Rosa's

1 Rosa's
MAP E4 ▪ 3420 W. Armitage Ave. ▪ 1-773-342-0452 ▪ Closed Sun & Mon ▪ www.rosaslounge.com

Though off the beaten path, the family-owned Rosa's is beloved citywide for its support of local artists, such as blues harpist Sugar Blue, and for the genuine welcome extended by its owners, Tony Mangiullo and his mother Rosa. The latter sometimes cooks for the patrons of this simple tavern.

2 Kingston Mines
MAP E2 ▪ 2548 N. Halsted St. ▪ 1-773-477-4646 ▪ www.kingstonmines.com

The largest of Chicago's blues joints, Kingston Mines packs its Lincoln Park locale with students, young professionals, and a broader spectrum of tourists. Two stages provide non-stop musical entertainment from 8pm to near 4am (5am on Saturdays). Acts range from homegrown house bands to national touring headliners. The kitchen serves up beer-sopping, finger-licking barbecue food.

3 B.L.U.E.S.
MAP E2 ▪ 2519 N. Halsted St. ▪ 1-773-528-1012

Among Chicago's many blues clubs, B.L.U.E.S feels the most like a Southern juke joint. Chalk it up to the narrow confines, loud sounds, and sweaty dancers. The club is just across the street from the popular Kingston Mines, but it's a better choice for older, more musically versed blues fans. Better yet, why not stop into both!

4 House of Blues
MAP K3 ▪ 329 N. Dearborn St. ▪ 312-923-2000 ▪ www.houseofblues.com

Folk art and exotic architectural remnants festoon the funky House of Blues. The vast 1,500-seat concert hall presents a variety of national touring acts from hard rock to hip-hop in addition to blues. The Sunday gospel brunch with sittings from 9:30am to noon is a must.

5 Jazz Showcase
MAP K5 ▪ 806 S. Plymouth ▪ 312-360-0234 ▪ Open 8pm–2am Mon–Sat, 4pm–2am Sun ▪ www.jazzshowcase.com

A slick, reasonably priced jazz club that has been around since 1947, the Jazz Showcase offers some of the finest jazz in the city. Performances at this 170-seat venue are diverse, with professionals as well as bands from university music programs.

6 Andy's Jazz Club
MAP K3 ▪ 11 E. Hubbard St.
▪ 312-642-6805

With its musical program that begins at lunchtime and continues into the evening, Andy's fills a void for those jazz fans who can't hold out for the late-night headliners. Prime perches at the horseshoe-shaped bar are much sought after in this no-fuss River North club.

7 Green Mill Cocktail Lounge
MAP E2 ▪ 4802 N. Broadway ▪ 1-773-878-5552 ▪ Limited DA

A former Prohibition-era speakeasy, Uptown's landmark Green Mill is a vintage treasure with a sweeping curved bar, vinyl booths, fading murals, and an authentic air of Chicago's gangster past. The city's premier jazz talents like Kurt Elling and Patricia Barber regularly play gigs here and Uptown Poetry Slam features every Sunday. It's out of the way but every cabbie in the city knows how to get there.

Green Mill Cocktail Lounge

8 Blue Chicago
MAP K2 ▪ 536 N. Clark St. & 736 N. Clark St. ▪ 312-661-0100 ▪ Open 8pm–1:30am Mon–Fri & Sun (to 2:30am Sat) ▪ www.bluechicago.com

Popular with tourists, Blue Chicago in River North operates two clubs located two blocks apart. Seats at both venues are few and far between, so come early if you need one, or be prepared to dance. The admission charge covers both clubs, which encourages bar hopping.

Buddy Guy headlining at his club

9 Buddy Guy's Legends
MAP L5 ▪ 700 S. Wabash Ave.
▪ 312-427-1190

A legend himself, bluesman Buddy Guy operates perhaps the best blues club in the city. The popular South Loop destination draws a mix of students, tourists, and local fans, particularly when Guy himself headlines (see p98).

10 California Clipper
1002 N. California Ave. ▪ 1-773-384-2547 ▪ www.californiaclipper.com

Home of the Purple Martini, this restored retro club, with a 40-ft (12-m) wooden bar and red-leather booths, bills itself as "the only bar with grape soda on its gun." Catch local, live country, dance, jazz, and blues from Thursday through Sunday (Monday is bingo night). See if you can spot "The Woman in White," the Clipper's elegant 1940s ghost.

Retro-style interior, California Clipper

🔟 Bars and Clubs

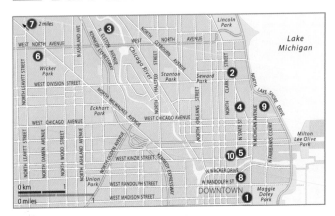

① Cindy's

On the rooftop of the Chicago Athletic Association Hotel, the stylish, glass-roofed Cindy's feels like a garden party from opening hours to close. A terrace with two firepits offers panoramic views of Millennium and Grant parks, and Lake Michigan. Cocktail choices include large-format dispensers designed for sharing (see p77).

A night out at the Zebra Lounge

② Zebra Lounge

An illegal speakeasy during Prohibition, this tiny piano bar has stood the test of time and competition, packing in loyal revelers nightly. Zebra prints dominate the decor, and martinis are the drink of choice. Singing along with the pianist to show tunes, torch songs, and oldies is expected (see p83).

③ Hideout

MAP D4 ▪ 1354 W. Wabansia Ave. ▪ 1-773-227-4433

Located off an industrial corridor on the Northside, Hideout is a popular destination for live music and arty performances. Many big names played here when they were rising stars, including Andrew Bird, and they often return. Events such as the Write Club pit debating scribes against one another.

④ Le Bar

MAP K2 ▪ 20 E. Chestnut St. ▪ 312-324-4000

In the beautiful Sofitel Hotel (see p116), a fashionable, over-30, mixed crowd fills this lobby lounge after work, lingering until the wee hours of the morning. Servers clad in black dispense martinis with scrumptious flavors such as chocolate and raspberry, and can cater to all tastes.

⑤ Sable Kitchen & Bar

MAP K3 ▪ 505 N. State St. ▪ 312-755-9704 ▪ Opening times vary

Named after Chicago's first non-native settler, Jean Baptiste Point du Sable (see p41), this dimly lit restaurant has a classic 1940s vibe to it. With its quintessential American dishes, interesting vegetarian options and an extensive appetizer list (which includes a range of delicious soups), Sable Kitchen & Bar is great for a lavish meal out.

6 The Violet Hour
MAP B4 ▪ 1520 N. Damen Ave. ▪ 1-773-252-1500

No sign marks the sophisticated Violet Hour in Wicker Park, a drape-swagged room that is Chicago's original artisan bar. Hostesses seat guests and waiting in line is common, but once ensconced in the exclusive high-backed chairs or booths, this is a great place to savor craft cocktails and lively conversation.

7 Billy Sunday
MAP B4 ▪ 3143 W. Logan Blvd. ▪ 1-773-661-2485

Chef Mathias Merges of nearby Yusho runs this upscale cocktail-focused bar located in Logan Square. If you're not familiar with bergamot bitters, Fernet or rhum agricole, it's best to quiz the creative mixologist. The bar also offers its own bottled and carbonated boozy sodas. A food menu of snacks and small plates keeps hunger pangs at bay.

8 Roof on the Wit
MAP K2 ▪ 201 N. State St. ▪ 312-239-9501 ▪ Closed Sun

Nestled amid the skyscrapers of the Loop, with spectacular views of the city, the winding "L", the Chicago River, and Lake Michigan, the Wit is a chic complex of lounge bars.

Snuggle by an open fire and take in the ultra-hip ambience and stunning vistas, with a cocktail in hand.

9 Drumbar
MAP L2 ▪ 201 E. Delaware Pl. ▪ 312-943-5000 ▪ Closed Sun & Mon

This stylish, contemporary rooftop bar offers great views of Chicago. An upscale nightclub with an innovative cocktail menu and a great wine list, Drumbar is a pricey yet classy establishment (dress code after 8pm).

Subterranean Three Dots and a Dash

10 Three Dots and a Dash
MAP K3 ▪ 35 N. Clark St. ▪ 312-610-4220

To find this hideaway, enter through the alley and descend to another time and place. Occupying several intimate rooms, this tiki bar includes a grass-thatch-fringed area serving pineapple-and-orchid-garnished drinks in classic tiki cups. Mai Tais and other cocktails pair well with *pupu platters* (island-style bar snacks).

Roof on the Wit, providing rooftop views over the city

🔟 Places to Eat

① Girl & the Goat
MAP H4 ▪ 809 W. Randolph St.
▪ 312-492-6262 ▪ $$$

Popular chef Stephanie Izard is the girl in Girl & the Goat. Though she offers goat and other bold-flavored dishes, there is a particular emphasis on vegetables, which make up a third of the menu. Reserve a table well in advance, or chance your luck and arrive at opening time (4:30pm).

② Alinea
Considered to be one of the world's foremost restaurants, Aliena has three Michelin stars and offers an exceptional gourmet experience. Chef Grant Achatz prepares tasting menus of highly creative New American dishes with wine or non-alcoholic pairings, served in three elegant dining areas with modern white and grey decor. The service is impeccable. Reserve well in advance (see p93).

③ Gibson's Steakhouse
MAP L2 ▪ 1028 N. Rush St.
▪ 312-266-8999 ▪ $$

Boisterous and convivial, Gibson's exudes a good time. A regular crowd of politicians, sports figures, and conventioneers packs the place nightly. The steakhouse fare is in every way a match to the atmosphere – big and bold. Huge lobster tails vie for attention with large slabs of beef. A reservation is critical, but for a more casual, walk-in experience try the burgers next door at Hugo's Frog Bar.

④ North Pond
Hidden from the road in leafy Lincoln Park, North Pond is a treasure – once you find it. Lodged in an Arts-and-Crafts-style building, the café offers an American seasonal menu with an emphasis on produce sourced in the Midwest.

Though dinner is the star, lunches of sandwiches, soups, and salads are equally creative and very well presented (see p93).

⑤ Spiaggia
Housed in an elegant tiered dining room, this upscale Italian restaurant has tables overlooking Oak Street Beach. It offers authentic, modern fare from award-winning chef Tony Mantuano, and a 700-bottle wine list. Café Spiaggia, its casual off-shoot at the same address, serves more rustic cuisine in relaxed yet stylish surroundings (see p83).

Spiaggia with floor-to-ceiling views

⑥ Blackbird
MAP J4 ▪ 619 W. Randolph St.
▪ 312-715-0708 ▪ Lunch 11:30am–2pm Mon–Fri, dinner 5–10pm Mon–Thu (to 11pm Fri & Sat) ▪ $$

Foodies and the fashion set both agree on Blackbird, a restaurant that sports minimalist decor and places the tables so close together that eavesdropping becomes part of the experience. Chef Paul Kahan generates the buzz, preparing sophisticated American dishes with French leanings. Menus change seasonally; reservations are essential.

Inventive fare, Blackbird

⑦ Next
MAP H3 ▪ 953 W. Fulton Market ▪ 312-226-0858 ▪ Closed Mon & Tue ▪ $$$

Founded by acclaimed chef Grant Achatz, Next reinvents itself each quarter with a new themed menu. Previous transformations include Paris Circa 1900, Childhood Memories, and Modern Chinese. Bookings are only sold through an advance ticketing system and sell out quickly, though resale options are often posted online.

⑧ Lou Mitchell's
MAP J4 ▪ 565 W. Jackson Blvd. ▪ 312-939-3111 ▪ No credit cards ▪ No dinner ▪ $

A classic diner in the Loop where the waitresses call you "Honey" and the coffee is bottomless, Lou Mitchell's has been around since 1923. Its trek-worthy meal is breakfast, highlighted by double-yolk eggs and homemade hash browns served in a skillet. Tables turn quickly and the staff doles out free donuts and candy with good cheer to those waiting in line.

⑨ Pizzeria Uno
MAP L3 ▪ 29 E. Ohio St. ▪ 312-321-1000 ▪ $

Uno's has been baking deep-dish pizza since 1943 – about as long as Chicagoans have debated whose pie is best. Its version comes several

Pizzeria Uno, a Chicago institution

inches deep, filled with cheese and toppings of your choice – truly a meal in one slice. The smallish Victorian brownstone strains under demand, sending the overflow up the street to its spin-off Pizzeria Due. Uno's individual pizza served at lunchtime is a real bargain.

⑩ Frontera Grill
Signature restaurant of chef Rick Bayless, Frontera Grill is credited with bringing authentic regional Mexican food – rather than Tex-Mex taco fare – stateside. Chili-roasted salsas and rich *moles* accompany grilled meats and delicious seafood. Since reservations are only available for parties of more than six, seats in the colorful, folk art-filled room go early as smaller groups try to avoid disappointment (see p83).

🔟 Shopping Destinations

1 State Street

A slew of chain stores line this legendary street (see p73), but it's the two old-time department stores that make it unique. The former Marshall Field's, now Macy's (see p76), here since 1907, has merchandise to satisfy every wealthy shopper's needs. At TJ Maxx the prices are lower, but the variety is still extensive (see p76).

Inside Macy's, State Street

2 Oak Street

MAP L1 ■ Borders: N. Michigan Ave. & Rush St.

If you have to ask how much it costs, you should probably plan on just window-shopping along this stretch of Chicago's upper-crust Gold Coast. Boutiques here sell designer wear, accessories, and shoes fit for a Paris runway – and include some shops exclusive to Chicago such as Tessuti (menswear) and Designs by Ming (custom clothing design).

3 Andersonville

MAP B3 ■ Clark St. between Foster and Bryn Mawr

This far Northside neighborhood hosts a string of independent boutiques along bustling Clark Street. Zoning regulations have kept out big-box stores with the result that the bookshops, galleries, design stores, and clothing specialists offer unique goods.

4 Bucktown Neighborhood

MAP B4 ■ Borders: Fullerton Ave. to Division Ave. & Kennedy Expressway to Western Ave.

Once a hotspot for starving artists, Bucktown and adjacent Wicker Park are now gentrified locales brimming with vintage clothes stores, edgy music shops, high-style designer boutiques, and antiques importers.

5 Bloomingdale's Home and Furniture Store

MAP K3 ■ 600 N. Wabash Ave. ■ Opening times vary ■ DA

This store's lovingly restored 1913 Moorish-style building is an attraction in its own right. Inside there's a sleek, four-level atrium with home decor departments that sell everything from bedding to furniture.

6 Broadway Antique Market

MAP E2 ■ 6130 N. Broadway ■ Open 11am–7pm, Mon–Sat, 11am–6pm Sun ■ DA

An old-time movie palace sign indicates the 1939 building that houses this market. With 85 dealers stocking artwork, jewelry, clothing, and more in styles such as Arts and Crafts, Art Deco, and Mid-Century Modern, you're sure to find something to suit.

Broadway Antique Market

7 Magnificent Mile

This stretch of North Michigan Avenue is one of the world's retail meccas. Besides sophisticated designer boutiques, there are malls (each with high-end department stores); and big-name chain and flagship stores (see pp32–3).

Retail heaven, Magnificent Mile

8 Architectural Artifacts

MAP B3 ■ 4325 N. Ravenswood Ave. ■ Open 10am–5pm daily
This sprawling warehouse on the Northside is chock-full of architectural and antique cast-offs, many from demolished buildings. Wares come from Chicago, Europe, and South America and range from massive stone mantles to neon signs and ceramic art tiles.

9 CAF Shop

MAP L6 ■ 224 S. Michigan Ave. ■ Open 9:30am–6:30pm Mon–Thu, 9am–7pm Fri, 9am–6:30pm Sat & Sun ■ DA
The CAF (Chicago Architecture Foundation) Shop, located in the historic Santa Fe Center (see p74), is part of the CAF's ArchiCenter, which also puts on exhibitions and runs city tours. Browse the shop for architecture and design-related books; art-glass panels and lamps in Frank Lloyd Wright designs; desk gadgets; and desirable kitchen gizmos.

10 Armitage Avenue

This tree-lined street in Lincoln Park (see p47) is a favorite for those who are seeking out-of-the-ordinary clothing, home decor, bath and body products – and don't mind spending more to get it.

TOP 10 CHICAGO SOUVENIRS

1 Frango Mints
Marshall Field's/Macy's (see p76) doesn't make these delicious mint chocolates anymore, but still sells them by the box-full.

2 Blues & Jazz CDs
CDs by Chicago music legends are on sale at the Water Works Visitor Information Center (see p80).

3 Vosges Haut Chocolat
The Chicago-based Vosges Haut Chocolat makes exotic velvety truffles with global flavors.

4 Art Poster
See the real thing, then buy a copy at the extensive Art Institute of Chicago gift shop (see p14).

5 Sports Jersey
Clubs T-shirts, Blackhawks sweaters, and Bulls jerseys make very popular apparel purchases.

6 Cubs Baseball Cap
Head to the Tribune Tower (see p80) gift shop for caps of the Major League team owned by the Chicago Tribune.

7 Art Glass
Take home a little Prairie style with a replica Frank Lloyd Wright art-glass panel from the CAF (Chicago Architecture Foundation) store.

8 Garrett's Popcorn
Garrett's Popcorn, especially the signature cheddar-caramel mix, is a classic Chicago guilty pleasure.

9 Sue Skeleton
Sue, the world's largest T. rex skeleton is far less menacing in mini model form from the Field Museum (see p18).

10 Chicago Snowglobe
Recall Chicago winters with a city skyline snowglobe from Accent Chicago in the Water Tower Place mall (see p32).

Chicago Blackhawks jersey

TOP10 Chicago for Free

1 Navy Pier
Navy Pier offers some of the best and most scenic strolling in the city. The pier is carnival-like, with myriad attractions begging you to spend money, but entry itself is free, as are the Wednesday and Saturday night firework displays in summer (see pp24–5).

2 Lincoln Park Zoo
Lincoln Park Zoo is one of the last free zoos in the country. There is no admission charge to see the apes, polar bears, birds, and more unusual animals. Daily sea lion feedings at 2pm are a great show (see pp30–31).

3 Public Art
Many famous artists, such as Pablo Picasso, Alexander Calder, and Marc Chagall have left their artistic mark on the city. Details of public art downtown are included in the Loop Sculpture Guide, downloadable from www.cityofchicago.org.

4 Lakefront Recreational Path
The 18-mile (29-km) paved path that runs along Lake Michigan is popular for running, cycling, skating, and walking. Many hotels offer rental bicycles and the city's bike-share program Divvy (see side bar) offers cheap wheels.

Blues festival for free at Grant Park

5 Free Events
Mayor's Office of Special Events (recorded info): 312-744-3370 ■ **www.cityofchicago.org/specialevents**
Summer in Chicago brings lots of free outdoor festivals, from the big music events of Grant Park, such as the Chicago Blues Festival (see p66), to parades, circuses in the parks, and neighborhood festivals that feature entertainment and vendors.

6 Comedy Shows
Comedy Sportz: 929 W. Belmont St.; 1-773-549-8080; www.comedysportzchicago.com ■ **iO Theater: 3541 N. Clark St.; 1-773-880-0199; www.ioimprov.com/chicago**
Chicago is the place to catch the best rising comedy and improv stars. The iO Theater runs dozens of shows each week from its Lincoln Park

Lakefront Recreational Path, great for strolling or cycling

headquarters, some of them free and all of them a blast. Also check Comedy Sportz for freebies.

7 Brewery Tours

Lagunitas Brewing: 2607 W. 17th St.; 1-773-522-2097; www.lagunitas.com ■ Revolution Brewing: 2323 N. Milwaukee Ave.; 1-773-227-2739; www.revbrew.com

Several microbreweries offer free tours of their facilities, including the sprawling Lagunitas Brewing in Pilsen. Tours begin in a recreation room with generous free samples, pinball machines, and other old-time amusements. Revolution Brewing in Logan Square also offers guided tours Wednesday to Sunday.

8 Free Museums

Seek out the smaller museums that offer free admission, including the National Museum of Mexican Art (see p44).

Millennium Park drawing a crowd

9 Millennium Park Programming

Over the summer, Millennium Park (see pp34–5) hosts a series of free events and performances, ranging from concerts by the Lyric Opera (see p54) and Chicago Children's Choir to screenings of popular movies.

10 Free Tours

The tourism bureau Choose Chicago (see p113) offers free guided tours led by locals. Sign up 10 days in advance via the website for a Chicago Greeter tour running for 2 to 4 hours. Or if you haven't planned ahead, InstaGreeters are available for 1-hour tours Friday to Sunday (see p114).

TOP 10 MONEY-SAVING TIPS

Chicago's popular Divvy bikes

1 Purchase half-price tickets for same-day theater performances at three Hot Tix booths. See www.hottix.org for shows available.

2 Many restaurants have good-value "Early Bird Specials" or pre-theater menus. Look for signs throughout the city advertising these deals.

3 Chicago's many beautiful parks offer free skating rinks, beaches, pools, tennis courts, and lots of walking and cycling paths.

4 Choose Chicago offers several promotions, such as Winter Delights, which include discounts on lodging, attractions, and meals; www.choosechicago.com.

5 CityPass grants entry to five top attractions including the Shedd Aquarium and Field Museum for 50 percent off; www.citypass.com.

6 Take unlimited 30-minute rides with one of the city's Divvy bikes. A day pass costs $9.95; www.divvybikes.com.

7 Ring the Loop aboard the Brown Line "L" running out to Lincoln Park and back again for a scenic tour at just $2.25 (see pp108–9).

8 Look for neighborhood restaurants that lack a liquor license and allow diners to bring their own beer or wine.

9 Skip the observatory at the John Hancock Center (see p79) and hit its 95th-floor Signature Lounge for equivalent views.

10 Visit the Chicago Cultural Center to see its stained-glass domes and to catch some of the free concerts that are regularly scheduled here (see p71).

🔟 Festivals and Events

① Chicago Blues Festival
MAP L6 ■ Late May–early Jun

The raucous weekend-long Blues Festival kicks off summer in Chicago. An estimated 750,000 listeners converge on Grant Park for the world's largest free blues event. The main stage hosts traditional bluesmen like Honeyboy Edwards, jazz interpreters such as Mose Allison, and blues-inflected artists like Bonnie Raitt. Smaller side stages offer a more intimate experience.

② Lollapalooza
MAP L6 ■ Late July
■ www.lollapalooza.com

The three-day rock festival known as Lollapalooza takes over Grant Park in late July. Major headliners such as Paul McCartney and Florence + the Machine are joined by emerging rockers, DJs, and techno innovators spread over several stages across the park. Passes go on sale, and usually sell out, in March.

③ Chicago Air and Water Show
312-744-3316 ■ Mid-Aug

This display of military power features historic aircraft flybys, a staged amphibious attack, and precision flying teams. Prime viewing spots are from Oak Street to Montrose Beach.

Chicago Jazz Festival

④ Chicago Jazz Festival
MAP L6 ■ 312-744-3316 ■ Late Aug/early Sep (inc. Labor Day weekend)

The Jazz Fest caps summer, when music fans are drawn to Grant Park for free concerts by greats like Branford Marsalis and Roy Hargrove.

⑤ Chicago Gospel Music Festival
MAP L6 ■ 312-744-3316 ■ Early Jun
■ www.choosechicago.com

For three days Grant Park resounds with stirring choirs and impassioned soloists. Headliners have included soul singer Al Green.

⑥ World Music Festival
312-744-3315 ■ Mid-Sep
■ www.worldmusicfestivalchicago.org

This city-wide, multi-venue, week-long festival showcases the very best

Chicago Air and Water Show

of traditional and contemporary international music. Concerts are low-cost or even free.

7 Magnificent Mile Holiday Lights Festival
MAP L2 ▪ Mid-Nov–end Dec

Merchants mark the start of the holiday season by lighting the shops, lampposts, and trees along Michigan Avenue. The parade and fireworks above the Chicago River on the Saturday night before Thanksgiving warrant braving the inevitable chill.

8 Taste of Chicago
MAP L6 ▪ Grant Park
▪ 312-744-3316 ▪ Late Jun–early Jul

Chicago's signature foods star during the nearly two-week-long Taste of Chicago. Musical entertainers, a carnival with rides, and cooking demonstrations entertain at the sprawling Grant Park event.

Entrance to Taste of Chicago

9 Old Town Art Fair
MAP F4 ▪ 1763 N. Park Ave.
▪ 312-337-1938 ▪ Jun ▪ Adm
▪ www.oldtownartfair.org

This 50-year-old fair installs 250 artist booths along Old Town's lanes. There are also food vendors, kids' entertainment, and garden tours.

10 Chicago Summer Neighborhood Festivals
312-744-3316 ▪ May–Sep
▪ www.choosechicago.com

Chicago has upwards of 100 neighborhood festivals. Virtually every summer weekend features an event or three, ranging from the gay-oriented North Halsted Market Days to the ethnic Korean Street Festival.

TOP 10 SPORTS TEAMS AND EVENTS

Chicago Bears in action

1 Chicago Cubs
Despite the Cubbies' losing streak, their baseball games at the Wrigley Field are often sell-outs *(see p87)*.

2 Chicago White Sox
Apr–Sep ▪ www.whitesox.com
The White Sox are renowned for their top-quality baseball.

3 Chicago Bears
Sep–Dec ▪ www.chicagobears.com
The football team generates rabid fans and tailgate picnics when in action on Soldier Field *(see p12)*.

4 Chicago Bulls
Oct–Apr ▪ www.bulls.com
Their basketball hasn't been the same since superstar Michael Jordan left.

5 Chicago Blackhawks
Oct–Apr ▪ www.chicago blackhawks.com
NHL ice hockey team sharing the United Center *(see p13)* with the Bulls.

6 Arlington Park
May–Sep ▪ www.arlingtonpark.com
Thoroughbred horses race at this park just north of Chicago.

7 Chicago Fire
Apr–Oct ▪ www.chicago-fire.com
Many local Latino soccer fans support the Fire.

8 Chicago Wolves
Oct–May ▪ www.chicagowolves.com
Four-time league champions offer a great evening of hockey.

9 Chicago Marathon
Oct ▪ www.chicagomarathon.com
40,000 entrants run through the city.

10 Chicago Triathlon
Aug ▪ www.chicagotriathlon.com
Over 6,000 run, bike, and swim in this action-packed one-dayer.

Chicago
Area by Area

Chicago's Gold Coast area fringed by Oak Street Beach

TOP 10 The Loop

Named for the ring of elevated train tracks that encircle it, this is downtown Chicago's core, and the city's financial and governmental hub. Abuzz with laptop-toting business folk during the week, the Loop is transformed on weekends when a veritable shopping frenzy erupts along its famous State Street. Those thirsty for culture come flocking to see the collections of the Art Institute of Chicago and to view the area's many architecturally significant buildings and its notable public art, while public parks offer green recreational spaces and the Riverwalk pedestrian path is a great place for strolling. The theater district, with its variety of shows, and the many great bars and restaurants give the area a lively nightlife.

Lion statue, the Art Institute of Chicago

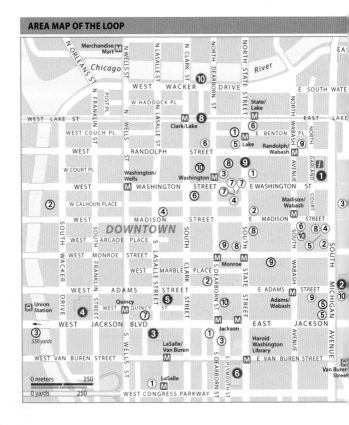

AREA MAP OF THE LOOP

1 Chicago Cultural Center

MAP L4 ▪ 78 E. Washington St.
▪ 312-744-6630 ▪ Open 9am–7pm
Mon–Thu, 9am–6pm Fri, 9am–6pm
Sat, 10am–6pm Sun ▪ Tours 1:15pm
Wed, Fri & Sat ▪ DA ▪ www.chicago
culturalcenter.org

Built in 1897 as the city's first main library, this magnificent Beaux-Arts building was described at the time as the "people's palace." In 1991, the library moved out, allowing several galleries, performance spaces and a visitor information center to move in. Guided tours offer a historical overview of the building, which occupies an entire block and has one of the world's largest domes, designed by L. C. Tiffany, and rooms modeled after the Doge's Palace in Venice and the Acropolis in Athens.

Tiffany Dome, Chicago Cultural Center

2 The Art Institute of Chicago

This extraordinary collection spans over 4,000 years of international art, much of it donated by wealthy Chicago collectors *(see pp14–15)*.

3 Chicago Board of Trade

MAP K5 ▪ 141 W. Jackson Blvd. ▪ Closed to the public until further notice

The Chicago Board of Trade (CBOT) was founded in 1848 to create a central marketplace in the fast-developing city, and moved to its current 45-story home in 1930. Designed by Holabird and Root, it is a stunning example of Art Deco. Capping the limestone building is a huge statue of Ceres, the Roman goddess of grain and harvest. A 23-story glass-and-steel addition designed by Helmut Jahn was added in 1980.

4 Willis Tower

An architectural superlative, the tower offers breathtaking views from its 103rd-floor Skydeck, where you'll find yourself on top of 222,500 tons of steel *(see pp12–13)*.

Willis Tower

WACKER DRIVE
NORTH STETSON
NORTH COLUMBUS DRIVE
ST STREET
AVE

Millennium Station

Millennium Park ❼

Maggie Daley Park
④

Monroe Harbor

EAST MONROE DRIVE
SOUTH LAKE SHORE DRIVE
SOUTH COLUMBUS DRIVE
DRIVE

Chicago Harbor

Grant Park ❼

⑤ The Rookery

MAP K4 ▪ 209 S. LaSalle St. ▪ Open 6am–6pm Mon–Fri (to 2pm Sat), closed Sun

This 11-story building, with its rusticated red granite base, was the country's largest office building and a precursor to modern skyscrapers when it was completed in 1888 by Burnham and Root (see p43). Its stunning skylit lobby was redesigned in 1907 by Frank Lloyd Wright (see pp36–7), who added a grand staircase and hanging light fixtures, both of which carry his signature circle-in-square motif.

Grand staircase, The Rookery

⑥ Harold Washington Library Center

MAP K5 ▪ 400 S. State St. ▪ Open 9am–9pm Mon–Thu, 9am–5pm Fri & Sat, 1–5pm Sun ▪ DA

Named after former city Mayor Harold Washington, Chicago's first African-American mayor, this is the largest public library building in the country. Its collections, which include a superlative Blues Archive and a vast children's library, fill an incredible 70 miles (110 km) of shelving. Architects Hammond, Beeby, and Babka incorporated architectural elements of several Chicago landmarks, such as The Rookery and The Art Institute of Chicago (see pp14–15) in the building's design: don't miss the ninth-floor Winter Garden atrium, which soars two stories to a spectacular glass dome.

Elevated train, the Loop

THE LOOP'S SCULPTURE

Setting a trend for public artwork downtown, Pablo Picasso's untitled sculpture, simply known as "the Picasso," was donated to Chicago in 1967. The Loop's street corners now accommodate more than 100 sculptures, mosaics, and murals by both established and upcoming artists. A guide to the open-air artworks can be downloaded from www.cityofchicago.org.

---

⑦ Millennium and Grant Parks

The modern Millennium Park (see pp34–5) is Chicago's superb adaptation of its "front yard." The park is home to a dynamic Frank Gehry-designed music pavilion and pedestrian bridge, and a vast sculpture by British artist Anish Kapoor. It also boasts lush gardens, restaurants, a winter ice rink, peristyle, and an interactive fountain by Spanish artist Jaume Plensa. The adjoining Grant Park (see p46) hosts many summer festivals including the Taste of Chicago (see p67). It is also home to Museum Campus (see p94), the Art Institute of Chicago (see pp14–17), and the ornate 1927 Buckingham Fountain.

⑧ The "L"

Originally called the Union Loop, this system of elevated trains came about after the 1871 Great Chicago Fire (see p40) when the city was rebuilt with such unexpected success that, within 20 years, its streets could no longer handle the influx of people, streetcars, and horses filling them. Today, four lines ring the business district – the

Orange, Purple, Pink, and Brown lines – with three others connecting it to places farther afield (see p52).

9 State Street
MAP K4 ■ From Wacker Dr. to Congress Parkway

This "great street" got its nickname from the 1922 hit song Chicago. Although it didn't always live up to this catchy moniker, it has won back many fans since its face-lift in 1996. It now sports replica Art Deco lampposts and subway entrances, and was listed on the National Register of Historic Places in 1998. This dynamic stretch has shopping, history, education, architecture, theater, and dining. The atmosphere is especially merry when the Thanksgiving parade brings Santa to town.

Enjoying the sunshine, Riverwalk

10 Chicago Riverwalk
MAP M3

Running along the south bank of the Chicago River, beginning near Lake Michigan, the Chicago Riverwalk is a waterside walkway that weaves under bridges. The pedestrian and bike path is a great place for spying the skyscrapers that line the river, and for picnicking. There are also restaurants, cafés, a floating garden, and boat and bike rentals. The section from State to LaSalle has amphitheater-like seating and an area for kayak launches.

A DAY IN THE LOOP

▶ MORNING

Start early with breakfast at the **Cherry Circle Room**, off the lobby in historic hotel the **Chicago Athletic Association** (see p117). Stroll across the street to **Millennium Park** (see pp34–5), to see the *Cloud Gate* sculpture, the video-screen fountains, and the Lurie Garden. From the park, take the pedestrian bridge designed by Renzo Piano directly to the **The Art Institute of Chicago**. A whirlwind tour of the highlights (see pp16–17), located on the upper level and in the Modern Wing, takes a couple of hours. Have lunch at **Terzo Piano** (see p77), on the 3rd floor of the Modern Wing, and enjoy panoramic views of Michigan Avenue and the the city's skyline.

AFTERNOON

Cross the street to the **Chicago Architecture Foundation**, which has a shop stocked with design-related souvenirs (see p63). Walk north along nearby **State Street**, stopping to browse the shops, until you reach the Chicago River. Spend an hour or two meandering along the **Chicago Riverwalk**.

EVENING

Book a pre-theater table at **Petterino's** (see p77), an old-school supper club, then check out the show at the **Goodman Theatre** (see p55) next door. Head back to the Chicago Athletic Association for a nightcap at **Cindy's** rooftop bar (see p77).

See map on pp70–71 ←

Architectural Sights

1 Monadnock Building
MAP K5 ■ 53 W. Jackson Blvd.

At 16 stories, this impressive Holabird and Roche designed building (1891) is one of the world's tallest all-masonry high-rises. Inside, there's a magnificent wrought-iron staircase *(see p43)*.

2 Marquette Building
MAP K4 ■ 56 W. Adam St.

Chicago architects Holabird and Roche built this Chicago School structure with a steel skeleton and decorative ornamentation in 1895.

3 Fisher Building
MAP K5 ■ 343 S. Dearborn St.

A Chicago School edifice with a steel structure, this 1896 Neo-Gothic building is by Daniel H. Burnham. Aquatic motifs on the façade honor the building's first owner, L. G. Fisher.

Art Deco features, One North LaSalle

4 One North LaSalle
MAP K4

This 1930-built, 49-story building was Chicago's tallest for 35 years, and is one of the city's best surviving examples of Art Deco architecture.

5 Santa Fe Center
Daniel H. Burnham designed this elegant high-rise in 1904: its carved building signs are from Chicago's days as a railroad hub. The ground level houses the Chicago Architecture Foundation *(see p63)*.

Beaux-Arts-style Chicago Theatre

6 Chicago Theatre
MAP K4 ■ 175 N. State St.

The red sign of this Beaux-Arts-style theater is a symbol of Chicago. Built in 1921 as a movie theater, today it is a performance venue.

7 Reliance Building
MAP K4 ■ 1 W. Washington St.

Daniel H. Burnham's stunning glass-and-white-glazed-terra-cotta building (1895) is now the Hotel Burnham *(see p117)*.

8 Sullivan Center
MAP K4 ■ 1 S. State St.

Eye-catching cast-iron swirls on part of the exterior of this building (1899 and 1903) express architect Louis H. Sullivan's love of elaborate detail.

9 Inland Steel Building
MAP K4 ■ 30 W. Monroe St.

One of the first skyscrapers to be built (in 1957) on steel, not concrete, pilings, this predates the John Hancock Center *(see p12)* in using external supports.

10 Federal Center
MAP K4 ■ 219 S. Dearborn St.

Flanked by Ludwig Mies van der Rohe's Modernist federal buildings, this plaza (1959–74) contains Alexander Calder's striking steel statue *Flamingo* (1974).

→ *See map on pp70–71*

The Best of the Rest

(1) Loop Theater District
MAP K4

A sidewalk plaque at Randolph and State streets denotes Chicago's officially designated Theater District, a cluster of old and new theaters.

(2) Civic Opera House
MAP J4 ■ 20 N. Wacker Dr.
■ www.lyricopera.org

This 1929 structure was inspired by Paris's Opera Garnier. It is home to the Lyric Opera of Chicago *(see p54)*.

(3) Old St. Patrick's Church
MAP J4 ■ 700 W. Adams St.

Chicago's oldest church (1856) is crowned by two towers – one Romanesque, one Byzantine – symbolizing East and West.

(4) Maggie Daley Park
MAP L4 ■ 37 E. Randolph St.

If Millennium Park is about art, its neighbor just to the east is all about play. Features include an elaborate children's playground, two climbing walls, tennis courts, and a popular frozen skating ribbon in winter.

(5) Symphony Center
MAP L4 ■ 220 S. Michigan Ave.
■ www.cso.org

At the heart of this center is Orchestra Hall (1904), the stunning home of the Chicago Symphony Orchestra *(see p54)*.

Orchestra playing, Symphony Center

(6) Chicago Temple
MAP J4 ■ 77 W. Washington St.

A Gothic-inspired structure designed by Holabird and Roche in 1923. Under the majestic spire is a 35-seat chapel.

(7) Federal Reserve Bank
MAP K4 ■ 230 S. LaSalle St.

This impressive edifice is one of 12 regional Reserve banks. When it was first built in 1922, it had the largest bank vaults ever constructed.

The logo of Chicago's Foodseum

(8) Foodseum Chicago
MAP K3 ■ 19 N. Dearborn St.
■ www.foodseum.org

This museum presents rotating exhibits devoted to food, often with a local bent, such as hot dogs and Chicago's role in popularizing them.

(9) Palmer House Hilton

The first Palmer House was destroyed in the Great Chicago Fire *(see p40)*. The current hotel is lavish, decorated with frescos, Tiffany light fixtures, and marble floors *(see p117)*.

(10) Daley Plaza
MAP K4

Home to the county court head-quarters, Daley Plaza is best known for its unnamed giant steel Picasso sculpture (1967) donated by the artist.

Shops

View from the upper floors, Macy's

1 Macy's
MAP K4 ■ 111 N. State St. ■ DA

Once Marshall Field's, Chicago's oldest and best-known department store is famous for its elaborate Christmas displays, dazzling Tiffany dome, and iconic clock. Established more than 100 years ago, it offers top clothing and homeware *(see p62)*.

2 TJ Maxx
MAP K4 ■ 11 N. State St. ■ DA

This department store offers a wide variety of clothing for adults and children. A great place to find quality brands at the cheapest prices.

3 Block 37
MAP K4 ■ 108 N. State St. ■ DA

The Loop's answer to the malls of the Magnificent Mile contains brands such as Sephora and Zara. Its Latin food hall is popular at lunch.

4 H&M
MAP K4 ■ 22 N. State St. ■ DA

This bargain store offers trendy clothes for all occasions, including a collection especially suited for teenagers and under-30s.

5 Old Navy
MAP K4 ■ 150 N. State St. ■ DA

This regional flagship store offers the ultimate Old Navy shopping experience, with two floors of discount jeans and T-shirts, and other casual comfort clothes.

6 Jewelers Center
MAP K4 ■ 5 S. Wabash Ave. ■ Closed Sun ■ DA

On the strip commonly known as "Jewelers Row" this 1912 Art Deco building contains over 180 jewelers. It is a friendly place to shop for gold, pearls, watches, diamonds, and gems at relatively low prices.

7 Nordstrom Rack
MAP K4 ■ 24 N. State St.

High style on sale at a fraction of the original prices lures bargain hunters to this charming little sister of the upscale and pricey Nordstrom.

8 Blick Art Materials
MAP K4 ■ 42 S. State St. ■ DA

This two-story family-owned store carries a wide range of cards, stationery and arty gifts in addition to its massive stock of fine art supplies.

9 Gallery 37 Store
MAP L4 ■ 66 E. Randolph St. ■ DA

Teenage artists involved in an arts training program create the incredible paintings, sculptures, and other artwork sold here. All proceeds from sales are returned to the program.

10 Iwan Ries & Co.
MAP L4 ■ 19 S. Wabash Ave. ■ Closed Sun ■ DA

Trading since 1857, this store sells a vast selection of cigars, pipes, and smoking accessories.

Places to Eat and Drink

PRICE CATEGORIES
Price categories include a three-course meal for one, a glass of house wine, tax, and a 15–20 percent tip.

$ under $30 $$ $30–$60 $$$ over $60

1 Everest
MAP K5 ■ 440 S. LaSalle St.
■ 312-663-8920 ■ Closed lunch, Sun & Mon ■ $$$

The restaurant on the top floor of the Chicago Stock Exchange has spectacular views and chocolate soufflé to die for.

2 The Gage
MAP L4 ■ 24 S. Michigan Ave.
■ 312-372-4243 ■ $$

Across from Millennium Park, this popular restaurant occupies a series of 19th-century millinery shops and has a vaguely Irish concept, serving Guinness on draft. The extensive menu highlights contemporary seasonal dishes.

3 Park Grill
MAP L4 ■ 11 N. Michigan Ave.
■ 312-521-7275 ■ $$

The only restaurant in Millennium Park, Park Grill would still be crowded even if it didn't try so hard. Its cooking, from burgers to salads and salmon *au poivre*, is superior.

4 Cherry Circle Room
MAP L4 ■ 12 S. Michigan Ave.
■ 312-792-3515 ■ $$

The restaurant in the Chicago Athletic Club offers intimate booths and antique furnishings. The equally stylish menu riffs on retro dishes, but with a creative modern twist and fresh seasonal produce.

5 Acanto
MAP L4 ■ 18 S. Michigan Ave.
■ 312-578-0763 ■ $$

From the owners of the neighboring Gage, Acanto, near Millennium Park, offers authentic Italian specialties from salumi to duck-egg spaghetti.

6 Petterinos
MAP K4 ■ 150 Dearborn St.
■ 312-422-0150 ■ $$

This pre- and post-theater Loop restaurant looks like an old-school supper club with its jacketed waiters, but it operates with modern efficiency. Good pastas and chops are on the menu, and the bar is a popular post-curtain haunt for actors.

Chic decor and great views at Cindy's

7 Atwood Café
MAP K4 ■ Hotel Burnham, 1 W. Washington St. ■ 312-368-1900 ■ $$
Expect top-notch hotel dining, where creative American cuisine leans toward comfort food.

8 Cindy's
MAP L4 ■ 12 S. Michigan Ave.
■ 312-792-3502 ■ $$
Crowds flock to rooftop Cindy's for the views over Millennium Park. Its menu caters to a convivial crowd, with sharable dishes such as seafood platters served at wooden picnic-inspired tables.

9 Russian Tea Time
MAP L4 ■ 77 E. Adams St.
■ 312-360-0000 ■ $$
A spirited taste of Russia, where the vodka flows freely and the beef stroganoff is a crowd-pleaser.

10 Terzo Piano
MAP L4 ■ 159 E. Monroe Dr.
■ 312-443-8650 ■ $
Located on the third floor of the Art Institute, Terzo Piano serves satisfying Italian café fare from chef Tony Mantuano of Spiaggia.

See map on pp70–71

TOP 10 Near North

History, culture, and commerce collide on Chicago's densely packed Near North side. This area is a pleasure to explore on foot, whether you are interested in shopping or fine art and architecture. The city's classiest shopping boulevard – the Magnificent Mile – bridges the posh 19th-century mansions of the lakeside Gold Coast (which has its own clutch of upscale boutiques) and the former industrial warehouses of River North, now mostly converted into art galleries. In addition to these, there are two local art museums. But ultimately, it's the Magnificent Mile on a Saturday that says more about Midwestern vitality and giddy American consumerism than any other Chicago experience.

AREA MAP OF NEAR NORTH

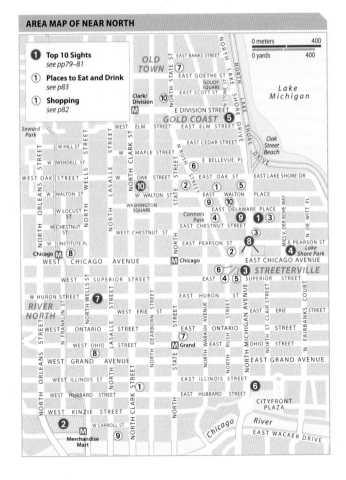

1 **Top 10 Sights**
see pp79–81

1 **Places to Eat and Drink**
see p83

1 **Shopping**
see p82

1 John Hancock Center

MAP L2 ■ 875 N. Michigan Ave.
■ Observatory open 9am–11pm daily,
Adm., DA ■ Signature Room open
daily, DA ■ www.johnhancock
centerchicago.com

Skidmore, Owings & Merrill
designed this 1970 landmark using
the signature Xs on the facade as
cross-braces to help the 1,100-ft
(335-m) building withstand the winds
coming off Lake Michigan. Soak up
the view from the 94th-floor
observation deck or drink it in from
the Signature Room restaurant and
lounge directly above. Many say you
get a better view from here than
from the South Side's Sears Tower –
and the lines are usually shorter too.

2 Merchandise Mart

MAP K3 ■ 222 W. Merchandise
Mart Plaza ■ DA

This massive two-square-block
edifice houses Chicago's premier
interior design trade showrooms.
When completed in 1930, the four
million-sq-ft (390,000-sq-m) building
was the largest in the world. Today, it
is second only to the Pentagon in
size, and is still the world's largest
commercial building. The Chicago
Architecture Foundation (see p63)
offers a 45-minute guided tour, which
is a great way to get to grips with this
daunting building.

Magnificent – or Mag – Mile

3 Magnificent Mile

Whether you're a shopper or
not, this store-lined strip warrants
a visit if only to get a feel for the
commercial pulse that seems to
keep Chicago humming (see pp32–3).

4 Museum of Contemporary Art

MAP L2 ■ 220 E. Chicago Ave. ■ Open
Tue–Sun 10am–5pm (to 8pm Tue)
■ Adm (free on Tue) ■ DA
■ www.mcachicago.org

One of the country's largest collections
of international contemporary art,
the MCA has over 6,000 objects, from
painting and sculpture to photography
and video installations. In summer,
the sculpture garden and displays of
performance art on the front lawn
enhance the experience.

The impressive stairwell, Museum of Contemporary Art

Aerial view, Gold Coast Area

5 Gold Coast Area
MAP K1

Chicago boasts many upscale neighborhoods, but none more historic and prestigious than the Gold Coast. Railroad, retail, and lumber tycoons built this elegant district in the decades following the Great Fire of 1871 (see p40), and its leafy streets are lined with 19th-century mansions interspersed with early 20th-century apartment buildings. There are no fewer than 300 designated historic landmarks in the Astor Street District alone, including buildings by Stanford White (such as 20 E. Burton Place), and Charnley House (1365 N. Astor Street), designed by Louis Sullivan (assisted at the time by Frank Lloyd Wright).

6 Tribune Tower
MAP L3 ■ 435 N Michigan Ave.

Topped by flying buttresses, this Gothic-style building was completed in 1925. Its faux-historic design had won a competition organized by Colonel Robert McCormick, publisher of the Chicago Tribune, the newspaper whose offices still occupy the building. Look closely at the facade, which is embedded with over 120 stones collected by correspondents from famed sights. There's a rock hailing from each of the 50 states, as well as fragments from international monuments such as Greece's Parthenon, India's Taj Mahal, and The Great Wall of China.

7 River North Gallery District
MAP K3 ■ Bounded by Merchandise Mart (south), Chicago Ave. (north), Orleans Ave. (west), Dearborn St. (east) ■ Chicago Gallery News: 312-649-0064; www.chicagogallerynews.com

Said to be the most concentrated art hub in the US outside of Manhattan, this district is jammed with galleries. Most are found in the handsome, 19th-century converted brick warehouses found alongside the "L" brown line. Huron and Superior streets are particularly worth a visit.

8 Chicago Water Works and Pumping Station
MAP L2 ■ Water Works and Pumping Station: 163 E. Pearson St. & 806 N. Michigan Ave. ■ Visitor Center: open 7:30am–7pm Mon–Thu; 312-337-0665; www.choosechicago.com ■ City Gallery: open 10am–6:30pm daily; 312-742-0808; DA

When the Great Fire of 1871 swept north, only the 1869 Water Works and Pumping Station escaped. Built by William W. Botington, the castellated Gothic-Revival Water Works was modeled after a medieval castle. It now houses the Chicago Visitor Center and the Lookingglass Theatre (see p55), and the fountain and chairs outside make it a focal point for street life. The functioning Pumping Station across the street houses the City Gallery, which specializes in photography.

Chicago Water Works

9 Fourth Presbyterian Church

MAP L2 ■ 126 E. Chestnut St.
■ Open 9am–5pm Mon–Sat,
7am–5pm Sun ■ DA

The first Fourth Presbyterian church, dedicated in 1871, celebrated its first sermon just hours before it was incinerated in the Great Fire. Rebuilt in 1914, today's church offers a peaceful respite from Magnificent Mile. Designed by Ralph Adams Cram, one of the architects behind New York's Cathedral of St. John the Divine, this church has a cathedral-like interior, with a splendid stained-glass west window. Free concerts take place on Fridays at noon.

Interior, Fourth Presbyterian Church

10 Newberry Library

MAP K2 ■ 60 W. Walton St.
■ 312-943-9090 ■ Open 9am–5pm
Mon–Fri (to 1pm Sat)

Founded in 1887 by wealthy Chicago businessman Walter L. Newberry, this research library is housed in a Romanesque-style granite building designed by architect Henry Ives Cob. It is stocked with rare books, maps, manuscripts, and music, and has research centers devoted to the history of cartography, American Indian and Indigenous studies, the Renaissance, and American history and culture. It also offers seminars on everything from Greek literature to genealogy research. The public can use the collections by applying for a reader's card free of charge.

A DAY IN THE NEAR NORTH

▶ MORNING

Line up early with the locals for a fortifying stack at **The Original Pancake House** (22 E. Bellevue Pl.). Afterward, stroll south on Rush Street to Oak Street. Take a left and walk the most exclusive shopping block in the city, where you can pop into stores such as Barneys New York. Once you hit Michigan Avenue, it's a short jaunt to the **John Hancock Center** (see p79) for sky-high views. Back on terra firma, cross the street to the **Chicago Water Works** for a close-up look at a piece of Chicago's history. Lovers of modern art should cross Michigan again and head to the **Museum of Contemporary Art** (see p79).

AFTERNOON

Everyone will get what they want for lunch at Foodlife, a food court on the second level of the mall in **Water Tower Place** (see p32). You can shop the seven floors of Chicago's first ever vertical mall, and then shop some more – and sightsee – along the **Magnificent Mile** (see pp32–3). If you've worked up an appetite, stroll over to **The Drake** hotel (see p117) for high tea, which is served until 5pm.

EVENING

Catch a show at Lookingglass Theatre, housed in the **Water Works Pumping Station**. Then head to chic NoMI in the **Park Hyatt Chicago** (see p83) for dinner and drinks with panoramic views of the landmark Water Tower and downtown Chicago.

See map on p78

Shopping

(1) Burton
MAP L2 ▪ 56 E. Walton St.
You don't have to be a snow boarder to shop at this flagship store, known for its range of funky boards and bold cold-weather gear.

(2) Barneys New York
MAP L1 ▪ 15 E. Oak St.
This branch of the Big Apple's downtown department store draws together the latest cosmetics, shoes, jewelry, accessories, and men's and women's apparel in a minimalist, open-plan, tri-level space.

(3) American Girl Place
MAP L2 ▪ Water Tower Place, 835 N. Michigan Ave.
▪ 1-877-247-5223
Parents of girls aged four to twelve make a beeline for this store, the only retail outlet of the American Girl line of dolls. A theater and café supplement three floors devoted to dolls, books, and other accessories.

American Girl Place

(4) Ikram
MAP L2 ▪ 873 N. Rush St.
Launched by a former Ultimo buyer, Ikram specializes in high-end women's fashion sold at top dollar. Chic wares and lines change seasonally, but shop assistance is uniformly personal.

(5) Polo Ralph Lauren
MAP L2 ▪ 750 N. Michigan Ave.
This massive four-story shop is so successful at transforming itself from a store to a den devoted to Ralph Lauren's to-the-manor-born lifestyle – note the horse and hound paintings throughout – that it warrants a visit from even the less well-heeled among us.

(6) Anthropologie
MAP K2 ▪ 111 E. Chicago Ave.
Women's apparel with a bohemian bent and housewares gathered from around the world sell briskly at this large, loft-like store.

(7) P.O.S.H.
MAP K3 ▪ 613 N. State St.
Recalling the days of elegant steamships and grand hotels, this store uses old-fashioned suitcases and steamer trunks to lovingly display vintage china and silverware engraved with hotel and ship logos.

(8) Paper Source
MAP J2 ▪ 232 W. Chicago Ave.
This arty River North shop is part art supply store, part stationer. The creative selection of cards and small gifts includes handmade stationery, cloth-covered sketchbooks, and novel desktop accessories.

(9) Original Penguin
MAP L2 ▪ 901 N. Rush St.
Famous for outfitting classic American icons such as Bing Crosby, this 1950s golf brand has a full range of men's and women's clothing.

(10) Bloomingdale's
MAP L2 ▪ 900 N. Michigan Ave.
An outpost of New York's homegrown department store that features in-store designer boutiques and a well-stocked shoe department.

Multi-level Bloomingdale's

Places to Eat and Drink

PRICE CATEGORIES
Price categories include a three-course meal for one, a glass of house wine, tax, and a 15–20 percent tip.

$ under $30 $$ $30–$60 $$$ over $60

Chefs at work, Nico Osteria

1 Frontera Grill
 MAP K3 ▪ 445 N. Clark St.
▪ 312-661-1434 ▪ Closed Sun & Mon
▪ Reservations only for groups of 5+
▪ $$

Chef Rick Bayless' regional Mexican cuisine warrants the two-margarita waits that inevitably face diners here.

2 NoMI
MAP L2 ▪ 800 N. Michigan Ave.
▪ 312-239-4030 ▪ $$$

On the seventh floor of the Park Hyatt Chicago, overlooking the landmark Water Tower, NoMI is a refined restaurant with a menu spanning sushi and steak.

3 Signature Lounge
MAP L2
▪ 875 N. Michigan Ave.
▪ 312-787-9596 ▪ $

Located on the 96th floor of the John Hancock Center, the Signature Lounge offers pricey cocktails and lofty views. No minors after 7pm.

GT Fish & Oyster

4 RL
MAP L2 ▪ 115 E. Chicago Ave.
▪ 312-475-1100 ▪ $$

This in-store steakhouse and power-eatery is furnished in upper-crust style by the Ralph Lauren Home shop while elegantly attired hostesses sport Polo.

5 Spiaggia
MAP L1 ▪ 980 N. Michigan Ave.
▪ 312-280-2750 ▪ $$

A special occasion restaurant, Spiaggia combines a romantic setting overlooking Oak Street Beach with sophisticated Italian food and a 700-vintage wine list.

6 Nico Osteria
MAP K1 ▪ 1015 N. Rush St.
▪ 312-994-7100 ▪ $$

This popular Italian seafood restaurant is run by famous chef Paul Kahan. The raw bar includes crudo and oysters.

7 Pump Room
MAP K1 ▪ 1301 N. State St.
▪ 312-229-6740 ▪ $$

A jazz trio, opulent decor, and a classic continental menu serve diners here. Celebrities love its famed "booth 1."

8 GT Fish & Oyster
MAP K3 ▪ 531 N. Wells St.
▪ 312-929-3501 ▪ $$

This seafood restaurant is one of the best in the city, providing elegant but unfussy food, including a raw bar and fixed-price offerings at lunch.

9 River Roast
MAP K3 ▪ 315 N. LaSalle St.
▪ 312-822-0100 ▪ $

Standing on the Chicago River, this bustling restaurant specializes in tasty roast chicken, served whole with crispy potatoes.

10 Zebra Lounge
MAP K2 ▪ 1220 N. State St.
▪ 312-642-5140

A classic piano lounge, the Zebra is intimate and decorated wall to wall in animal prints. It's a funky place to drink cocktails in the Gold Coast.

See map on p78

TOP 10 Northside

Encompassing parts of Old Town, Lincoln Park, Lakeview, and Wrigleyville, Chicago's Northside boasts upscale restaurants and chi-chi boutiques galore, as well as some of the city's best bars and one of its most progressive theater companies, the Steppenwolf *(see p88)*. Older buildings have been transformed into beautiful condominiums, while stylish new apartments are springing up on empty lots. In season, nearby Wrigley Field fans bolster the lively Wrigleyville atmosphere by swarming the surrounding streets and bars. The vibrant gay hub of "Boystown" is also in this area, while running along Northside's eastern border is the incredible lakefront.

Rainbow pillar in Boystown

AREA MAP OF NORTHSIDE

1 Top 10 Sights
see pp87–9

1 Restaurants
see p93

1 Shops
see p90

1 Neighborhood Bars
see p92

1 Gay and Lesbian Bars
see p91

Previous pages Tiffany Dome, Chicago Cultural Center

Chicago Cubs playing to a full house, Wrigley Field

1 Wrigley Field

MAP D1 ■ 1060 W. Addison St.
■ 1-773-404-2827 ■ Tours daily, $25
■ Adm ■ DA ■ www.cubs.com

Built in 1914, this is the USA's oldest National League baseball park. The home team, the Chicago Cubs, haven't won a World Series championship since 1908 (before the field even existed), but that doesn't stop Northsiders from being behind them every step of the way. In season (March–September), spending an afternoon cheering on the "Cubbies" in this marvelous stadium, with its ivy-clad walls, is a quintessential Chicago experience.

2 Chicago History Museum

MAP F4 ■ 1601 N. Clark St.
■ Open 9:30am–4:30pm Mon–Sat,
noon–5pm Sun ■ Adm ■ DA

Focusing on Illinois and Chicago history since settler days, this museum was established in 1856 and is the city's oldest cultural institution. One of the society's first donors bequeathed his collection of Lincoln memorabilia: the ex-president's deathbed is one of the items displayed. Visitors can climb aboard the Pioneer locomotive, while events such as the World's Columbian Exposition and the Great Chicago Fire (see p40), are brought to life by photographs, decorative arts, and other exhibits. There is also a collection of costumes from the mid-18th century to the present, belonging to famous figures, from George Washington to Michael Jordan.

3 Boystown

MAP E1–2 ■ N. Halsted St.
(& much of Broadway) from Belmont Ave. to Grace St., & Clark St. from Belmont to Addison Aves

Strolling down North Halsted Street, it's fairly evident you're in Chicago's gay neighborhood when you hit shops called Gay Mart and Cupid's Treasure. Just 30 years ago, this area – officially East Lakeview – was pretty shabby, the bars were without signs, and parking was a cinch. But now buzzing Boystown is gay central – by day and by night.

Peggy Notebaert Nature Museum

4 Peggy Notebaert Nature Museum

MAP F3 ■ 2430 N. Cannon Dr. ■ 1-773-755-5100 ■ Open 9am–5pm Mon–Fri, 10am–5pm Sat & Sun ■ Adm ■ DA

This museum's sloping, beige exterior was inspired by the sand dunes that once occupied its site. Inside are a host of engrossing interactive exhibits, the highlight being the walk-through Butterfly Haven.

5 Armitage/Halsted Shopping District

MAP E4 ■ Armitage Ave. from Halsted St. to Racine Ave., & Halsted St. from Webster to Armitage Aves

This area of unique boutiques is a boon for fashionistas. Dozens of shops here sell everything from sophisticated evening wear to high-end accessories. Many of the stores occupy renovated Victorian town homes, which are set along pretty, tree-lined streets.

6 Lincoln Park Conservatory

MAP F3 ■ 2391 N. Stockton Dr. ■ Open 9am–5pm daily ■ DA

Take a free trip to the tropics at this spacious conservatory, just next to Lincoln Park Zoo. Opened in 1893, the glass structure is a year-round, 80° F (40° C) sanctuary from Chicago's bustle, and offers a welcome respite from the city's long winters. Paths meander past lush palms, flourishing ferns, and exquisite 100-year-old orchids. Avoid the crowds by coming on a weekday when, unless a seasonal show is taking place, it's a quiet space, with trickling water as the only background sound.

Lion enclosure, Lincoln Park Zoo

7 Lincoln Park Zoo

Who's watching who at this beloved city zoo, which attracts more than three million visitors annually *(see pp30–31)*.

8 Steppenwolf Theatre Co.

MAP E4 ■ 1650 N. Halsted St. ■ 312-335-2650 ■ www.steppenwolf.org

Founded in 1974 in a church basement, this theater company grew quickly to include a corps of actors who would become famous on stage and screen, including John Malkovich and Gary Sinise. Now based in a modern complex with two full stages and a smaller Garage Theater, Steppenwolf has sent many hits to New York's Broadway over the years.

Lush gardens in front of Lincoln Park Conservatory

9 North Avenue Beach

MAP F4 ■ Lakeshore Dr. &
North Ave. ■ Open dawn to dusk
■ Lifeguards on duty from Memorial
Day–Labor Day

When summer graces Chicago with
its presence, locals of all ages and
nationalities converge on this short,
but inviting beach. Running along its
edge is the lakefront path, where
cyclists, in-line skaters, runners, and
walkers stream by. Confident folks
strut their stuff at the outdoor gym,
sand volleyball courts allow the
energetic to let off steam, and the
rooftop bar of the steamship-shaped
beach house is perfect for a drink
while watching the activity below.

Jogging, North Avenue Beach

10 Second City

MAP F4 ■ 1616 N. Wells St. ■
312-337-3992 ■ www.secondcity.com

It's hard to overstate the influence
that Second City has had on comedy
in America since it opened its doors
at North Wells Street in 1959. The
home of improvisational comedy,
Second City has been the starting
point for an army of talent from
John Belushi and Bill Murray to
Tina Fey, Dan Aykroyd, and Stephen
Colbert, and entire casts of the
popular TV show *Saturday Night Live*.
On two stages at its headquarters in
Old Town, Second City offers full-
length shows (another venue, UP
Comedy Club on West North Avenue,
is reserved for stand-up comedy).
Improv seating is first come first
served and tight, which just makes
the hilarity even more contagious.

MORNING

Fuel up for the day at one of
Lincoln Park's favorite breakfast
joints, **Frances'** (2552 N. Clark
St.), where they serve a
wonderfully fluffy French toast.
Afterwards, take a stroll east
down Wrightwood Avenue and
keep walking until you come to
the **Lincoln Park Zoo** (see pp30–
31), where you can ride on the
wild side on the African Safari
motion simulator. Then meet all
the animals before breaking for
lunch with a view at **Café Brauer**,
built in 1908 by Prairie School
architect Dwight Perkins.

AFTERNOON

During warm weather, head to
the lakefront along Fullerton
Avenue where you can stroll, rent
bikes, sunbathe, or even brave
the chilly Lake Michigan waters.
In colder months, catch a bus
(nos. 22 or 151) and immerse
yourself in the **Chicago History
Museum** (see p87), or take a five-
minute cab ride to **Armitage/
Halsted Shopping District** (see
p88) for classy retail therapy.

EVENING

This part of town has an
abundance of good eateries: hop
the "L" four stops or cab it to try
Mia Francesca's (see p93), a lively
Italian trattoria where the pasta
dishes are big enough for two,
and there's an excellent wine list.
Round off your day with a visit to
Kingston Mines (see p56) – just a
short cab-ride away – to hear some
of the city's best blues musicians.

See map on p86e ←

Shops

1 Architectural Artifacts

MAP B3 ▪ 4325 N. Ravenswood Ave.

This huge warehouse stocks cast-offs from period homes, factories, and offices. Interesting pieces, from old wooden doors to models used to make rubber gloves, offer a down-the-rabbit-hole retail experience.

2 Paper Source

MAP D1 ▪ 3543 N. Southport Ave.

Originally an artist's supply store, Paper Source now concentrates on stationery and paper goods, from origami papers and individual handmade gift-wrap sheets to stylish notecards and greeting cards. A craft area offers workshops in card making.

3 Lori's Designer Shoes
MAP E4 ▪ 824 W. Armitage Ave.

Devoted shoe hounds flock to this Lincoln Park store for its hot styles at discounted prices. The floors and walls are stacked high with boxes for handy self-serve try-on access.

4 Art Effect

MAP E4 ▪ 934 W. Armitage Ave.

An institution on trendy Armitage Avenue since 1984, this eclectic boutique offers a little bit of everything, from offbeat fashions, accessories and statement jewelry to retro kids' toys and unusual homewares.

A quirky item for sale at Art Effect

5 Beatnix

MAP E2 ▪ 3400 N. Halsted St.

This store boasts the best supply of costumes and vintage gear in the city, including wigs, distinctive mod jewelry, and make-up.

6 Andersonville Galleria
MAP B3 ▪ 5247 N. Clark St.

Artists, jewelers, fashion designers, knitters, and more maintain booths

Unabridged Bookstore

at Andersonville Galleria, a creative co-op. You could easily spend a few hours wandering around the three-story maze.

7 Unabridged Bookstore

MAP E2 ▪ 3521 N. Broadway

Known for its large gay and lesbian section, this Boystown (see p87) bookstore also stocks books of all types, particularly kids' and Spanish-language books.

8 Scout Chicago

MAP B3 ▪ 5221 N. Clark St.

An antique shop with a funky flare for mid-century modern and industrial one-offs, Scout always stocks surprises such as old gym lockers, in cramped but intriguing quarters.

9 Uncle Dan's
MAP D1 ▪ 3551 N. Southport Ave.

An outdoors equipment store with urban style that offers everything from mummy bags and tents to street-smart parkas that won't make you look like the Michelin man. There's a great selection of backpacks, too.

10 Brimfield

MAP B3 ▪ 5219 N. Clark St.

Another of Andersonville's stylish vintage shops, Brimfield specializes in woolly plaids, from throw blankets to upholstered armchairs. Retro decorative items make browsing fun.

Gay and Lesbian Bars

1 Second Story Bar
MAP L3 ■ 150 E. Ohio St.

This intimate bar that serves stiff drinks is a great evening escape. Its friendly atmosphere (and small size) encourages visitors to mix.

2 The Closet
MAP E2 ■ 3325 N. Broadway

This dance club attracts a mostly lesbian crowd, but gay men and straight couples also groove to R&B, rap, dance, and diva videos.

3 Roscoe's Tavern
MAP E2 ■ 3356 N. Halsted St.

A young, preppy set packs this neighborhood bar for its antique decor, cozy fireplace, cheesy dance tunes, and, in summer, beer garden.

4 Sidetrack
MAP E2 ■ 3349 N. Halsted St.

Find some of the best cruising at this vast, four-room bar with more than two dozen video monitors that highlight a different theme (like show tunes or 1980s music) every night.

5 Kit Kat Lounge & Supper Club
MAP E2 ■ 3700 N. Halsted St. ■ Open dinner daily, Sun brunch

Martinis come in 52 flavors at this chic spot, where female impersonators show their lip-synching talent.

6 Big Chick's
MAP B3 ■ 5024 N. Sheridan Rd.

In a world of LGBT bars dominated by men, Big Chick's welcomes all persuasions. Themed events include trivia night and Bear Den night.

7 Berlin
MAP E2 ■ 954 W. Belmont Ave.

This edgy club attracts every type from straight girls to drag queens. After midnight, the dance floor hits its peak, rocking with a stellar sound system and light show.

8 Progress Bar
MAP E2 ■ 3359 N. Halsted St.

This sleek lounge is ideal for sipping must-try martinis while Boystown people-watching through wall-to-wall windows.

9 Crew Bar & Grill
MAP E2 ■ 4804 N. Broadway

With 20 enormous HDTVs, you'll always find a good spot to catch a game at this premier gay sports bar.

10 Hydrate
MAP E2 ■ 3458 N. Halsted St.

Hydrate features a bar in front with roll-up garage-style doors, and a dance floor out back that cranks into the early hours. A drag queen show "Beautie and Beaus" takes place on Saturday nights.

Pink lighting sets the mood, Kit Kat Lounge & Supper Club

See map on p86

Neighborhood Bars

Popular brewery Goose island

1 Goose Island
MAP D4 ■ 1800 N. Clybourn Ave.

Though now owned by a brewing giant, Chicago's original microbrewery remains a local favorite, with a range of beer styles and a full menu to match. Brewery tours are offered on Saturday and Sunday.

2 Schubas Tavern and Harmony Grill
MAP D1 ■ 3159 N. Southport Ave.

Twenty-somethings dress down for beer, live music, and a great restaurant that packs in crowds, especially on the patio during warm-weather weekends.

3 Murphy's Bleachers
MAP E1 ■ 3655 N. Sheffield Ave.

Located just beyond the Wrigley Field, Murphy's Bleachers has a loyal following among Cubs fanatics as well as fair-weather drinkers.

4 Southport Lanes & Billiards
MAP D1 ■ 3325 N. Southport Ave.

During the day, this is a laid-back bar: at night, a rowdy young crowd take turns at the four hand-set bowling lanes.

5 Village Tap
MAP D1 ■ 2055 W. Roscoe St.

Popular for its seasonal back patio, the Village Tap in laid-back Roscoe Village offers a strong selection of tap beers and a good bar menu.

6 Gingerman Tavern
MAP D1 ■ 3740 N. Clark St.

A Wrigleyville stalwart, Gingerman is not a sports bar despite being in the home of the Chicago Cubs . It has a range of beers and a few pool tables.

7 Delilah's
MAP D2 ■ 2771 N. Lincoln Ave.

Declared one of "the great whiskey bars in the world" by *Whiskey Magazine*, Delilah's has been a neighborhood watering hole for years. It has some 400 different types of whiskeys on offer, not to mention many beers on tap.

8 Huettenbar
MAP B3 ■ 4721 N. Lincoln Ave.

In the historically German district of Lincoln Square, Huettenbar channels old-world *gemeuthlichkeit*, or warmth, with flower-box-trimmed front windows, German beer on tap, and an Alpine mural behind the bar.

9 Half Acre Tap Room
MAP E3 ■ 4257 N. Lincoln Ave.

The popular microbrewer Half Acre operates a neighborly taproom that usually features about 10 beers on tap for tasting. Guests can also get pitchers to go.

Cozy interior, Half Acre Tap Room

10 The Tin Lizzie
MAP E3 ■ 2483 N. Clark St.

A sports bar-and-dance club, Tin Lizzie is packed wall-to-wall with twenty- to thirty-somethings most weekend nights, when DJs spin a variety of tunes.

Restaurants

PRICE CATEGORIES
Price categories include a three-course
meal for one, a glass of house wine, tax,
and a 15–20 percent tip.

$ under $30 $$ $30–$60 $$$ over $60

1 Alinea
MAP E4 ■ 1723 N. Halsted St. ■
312-867-0110 ■ Closed lunch, Mon &
Tue ■ DA (mention in advance) ■ $$$
This high-end, fine-dining restaurant
serves delicious unique food pairings
in a very stylish setting.

2 Mia Francesca
MAP F4 ■ 3311 N.
Clark St. ■ 1-773-281-3310
■ Open dinner daily,
10am–3pm Sat & Sun ■ $$
The wait for the generous
portions of flavorful pastas,
seafood, and chicken at this
lively eatery is worth it.

3 Geja's Café
MAP E4 ■ 340 W.
Armitage Ave. ■ 1-773-281-
9101 ■ Closed lunch
■ No DA ■ $$
The ultimate fondue in a
romantic setting. Choose cheese
or hot oil, or just opt for the divine
chocolate fondue.

4 Fish Bar
MAP E2 ■ 2956 N. Sheffield
■ 1-773-681-8177 ■ Open 11:30am–
10pm Sun–Thu (to 12am Fri & Sat)
■ $$
This small eatery serves the best
fish in the city – everything from
salmon, oysters, and tilapia to
classic fish and chips.

5 Yusho
MAP B4 ■ 2853 N. Kedzie Ave.
■ 1-773-904-8558 ■ Closed lunch
(except Sun) ■ $$
Highly regarded chef Mathias
Merges runs this casual Japanese
tavern with serious food ambitions.
Try the twice-fried chicken.

6 Longman & Eagle
MAP B4 ■ 2657 N. Kedzie Ave.
■ 1-773-276-7110 ■ Open from 9am
daily ■ $$
This funky place takes its farm-fresh
fare seriously but has a casual
atmosphere in two packed rooms.
No reservations; arrive early or wait.

7 North Pond
MAP F3 ■ 2610 N. Cannon Dr.
■ 1-773-477-5845 ■ Open Wed–Sun
from 5:30pm, and Sun brunch ■ $$
This pond-side restaurant (a former
skaters' "warming house") serves up
American gourmet cuisine.

North Pond's beautiful dining room

8 Lula Café
MAP E4 ■ 2537 N. Kedzie Ave.
■ 1-773-489-9554 ■ Open 9am–2am
Wed–Mon ■ $
An eclectic café in Logan Square,
Lula champions local and organic
ingredients in its farm-to-table meals,
from breakfast through to late night.

9 Ann Sather
MAP E2 ■ 909 W. Belmont Ave.
■ 1-773-348-2378 ■ $
Known for its scrumptious
breakfasts, this Swedish restaurant
also serves lunchtime specialties.

10 Boka
MAP E4 ■ 1729 N. Halsted St.
■ 312-337-6070 ■ Open from 5pm
daily ■ $$
Boka offers elegant, seasonally
informed food in a series of rooms.

See map on p86

TOP 10 South Loop

Just south of the business-centric Loop, this sprawling area mixes ethnic enclaves such as Chinatown (founded in the 1870s by migrant transcontinental railroad workers) with upper crust addresses, built after the Great Chicago Fire of 1871 *(see p40)*. The region has many Chicago "must-sees," but the jewel in the crown is undisputedly the impressive Museum Campus: here, the Field Museum, John G. Shedd Aquarium, and Adler Planetarium celebrate the wonders of the earth, sea, and sky respectively, collectively drawing over four million visitors each year. The highway that once separated the Field from its neighbors has been replaced by an inviting green campus, where cyclists and skaters join museum-goers on the plant-bordered paths in fair weather.

Figurine, Field Museum

Skeleton exhibits, Field Museum

1 Field Museum
One of the three lakefront institutions to occupy the Museum Campus, the vast Field Museum boasts a collection of more than 20 million fascinating natural history and anthropological artifacts from around the world *(see pp18–19)*.

2 Prairie Avenue District
MAP C5 ▪ For walking tours (Jul–Sep) call 312-326-1480 ▪ Clarke House: 1827 S. Indiana Ave.; tours noon & 2pm Wed–Sun; adm; DA ▪ Glessner House: 1800 S. Prairie Ave.; tours 1 & 3pm Wed–Sun; adm; no DA
Of the wealthy enclaves both north and south of the Chicago River that

AREA MAP OF SOUTH LOOP

1 Top 10 Sights
see pp94–7

1 Places to Eat
see p99

1 Bars and Clubs
see p98

grew up following the Great Fire of 1871, Prairie Avenue was the most fashionable and ritziest. Only a few mansions remain today, of which two are open to the public (tour only): the Romanesque-Revival 1887 Glessner House, and Chicago's oldest building – Clarke House – built in 1836.

3 Blues Heaven Foundation

MAP C5 ■ 2120 S. Michigan Ave.
■ For tours call 312-808-1286
■ Closed Sun ■ Adm ■ Limited DA

Located in the former studios of Chess Records, where blues greats from Muddy Waters to Willie Dixon once recorded, Blues Heaven has records, photos, and stage costumes dedicated to Chicago's blues style and its performers. The former label's music plays on the PA. There are occasional live performances.

Wild Reef exhibit, John G. Shedd Aquarium

4 John G. Shedd Aquarium

The second of the three Museum Campus sights, the Shedd is also one of the oldest and most visited public aquariums in the world. Dive in to discover the many treasures of the aquatic world on show (see pp28–9).

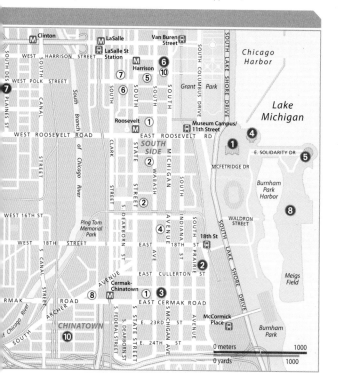

Star gazing, Adler Planetarium

5 Adler Planetarium
MAP M6 ■ 1300 S. Lake Shore Dr.
■ Open 9:30am–4pm Mon–Fri,
9:30am–4:30pm Sat & Sun; third Thu
of month 6–10pm for "Adler After
Dark" (over-21s only); for showtimes
call 312-922-7827 ■ Adm ■ DA

The first planetarium in the Western
Hemisphere completes the Museum
Campus trio. Visit its numerous
galleries to walk among the stars,
explore the worlds that orbit the Sun,
and be enlightened by 1,000 years of
astronomical discovery. Don't miss
the Sky Theater show, which is
projected on the 68-ft (21-m) dome
of the historic Zeiss planetarium. The
virtual reality events in the StarRider
Theater launch you into the outer
reaches of space and even give you
the chance to interact with the show
via a panel in the armrest.

6 Museum of Contemporary Photography
MAP L5 ■ 600 S. Michigan Ave. ■ Open
10am–5pm, Mon–Sat (to 8pm Thu),
noon–5pm Sun ■ DA ■ www.mocp.org

Run by and located in Columbia
College Chicago, this museum is one
of a kind in the Midwest. It exhibits
the portfolios of international modern
masters, with shows tending toward
the experimental rather than the
traditional documentary. Changing
exhibitions also present a mixture of
local talents and well-established
ones, such as Gary Winogrand and
William Eggleston. Frequent gallery
talks give curators and artists the
chance to discuss the shows with
museum-goers.

7 Maxwell Street Market
MAP J6 ■ 548 W. Roosevelt Rd.
■ Open 7am–3pm Sun

Both 19th-century European
immigrants and 20th-century African-
American settlers fleeing the Deep
South got their entrepreneurial start
selling from pushcarts around
Maxwell Street. In 1994 the market
was relocated to make way for the
new University of Illinois at Chicago
and, while a shadow of its former self,
it still makes for a vibrant Sunday
morning. Do expect plenty of
Mexican housewares and used tools.
The occasional treasure, such as a
vintage fur coat, does show up,
however. Another reason to visit is to
try the homemade tacos from the
Mexican food stalls that line the street.

8 Northerly Island
MAP M6 ■ 1521 S. Linn White
Dr. ■ 312-745-2910 ■ Open 6am–
11pm ■ www.chicagoparkdistrict.com

Northerly Island was part of city
planner Daniel Burnham's plan for
the lakefront to include a series of
offshore islands acting as parks. At
Northerly Island, Burnham's vision
is now a reality. The green space
extending south of the Adler
Planetarium is the city's newest
lakefront park, which hosts native
gardens carved with walking trails,
and an outdoor concert stage.

Lakefront strolling, Northerly Island

(9) Jane Addams Hull House

MAP H5 ▪ 800 S. Halsted St.
▪ 312-413-5353 ▪ Open 10am–4pm
Tue–Fri, noon–4pm Sun ▪ DA
▪ www.hullhousemuseum.org

When European immigrants were flooding Chicago to work in its rail and stock yards during the late 19th and early 20th centuries, Jane Addams bought Hull House for a specific purpose. From here, she offered social services and facilities to this immigrant working class, including day care, employment counselling, and art classes. Winner of the 1931 Nobel Peace Prize, Addams also championed the rights of women and helped usher in child labor laws. Her office, furnishings, and artwork are on display, and temporary exhibits tell the story of the settlement at Hull House and the invaluable work of its residents.

The famous Chinatown Gate

(10) Chinatown

MAP B5 ▪ Around Wentworth
Ave. & Cermak Rd.

Crowned by the landmark Chinatown Gate spanning Wentworth Avenue, Chicago's Chinatown isn't that large – running roughly eight blocks – but it is colorful. Home to Chicago's oldest Asian community, Chinatown was founded in the 19th century by transcontinental railroad workers fleeing West Coast prejudice. Cantonese and Mandarin are still spoken far more widely here than English. Stroll Wentworth to see the ornate On Leong Tong Building, buy fresh almond cookies from Chinese bakeries, peruse the many import and herbal shops, or dine in one of the numerous local restaurants.

EXPLORING SOUTH LOOP

▶ MORNING

Start by grabbing coffee and an oreo cookie flapjack at **The Bongo Room** (1152 S. Wabash Ave., 312-291-0100). From there, walk through Grant Park to Museum Campus. Here you can choose between the **Field Museum** (see pp18–19), **Adler Planetarium**, and **John G. Shedd Aquarium** (see pp28–9). If you plan to visit other museums on your trip, it makes sense to purchase a CityPass (see p65). If you opt to see the highlights of each, end up at the Shedd, where the **Soundings** restaurant offers good food and great views overlooking the lake.

AFTERNOON

Hail a cab (plenty wait outside the museums) or walk to the nearby pedestrian bridge at 18th Street to get to the **Prairie Avenue District** (see pp94–5), where you can stroll the historic streets and maybe even catch the 3pm tour of the **Glessner House** (see p95). Muster energy to catch a cab to the **Adler Planetarium** and walk south, enjoying the skyline views from **Northerly Island**.

EVENING

Head over to Wabash Avenue for an early supper at one of the trendy eateries on what is now a burgeoning strip. A popular spot is **Gioco** (see p99), known for its stellar Italian fare (reservations are recommended). After dinner, go on to **Buddy Guy's Legends** (see p98) and hear the blues.

See map on pp94–5 ←

Bars and Clubs

1 Reggie's
MAP K6 ▪ 2105 S. State St.

This rock venue and grill-pub offers nightly musical entertainment and good bar fare. Next door, Record Breakers sells rare vinyl and CDs.

2 M Lounge
MAP K6 ▪ 1520 S. Wabash Ave.

Listen to traditional and modern jazz in style on comfy couches and low-slung seating in cranberry, chocolate, and sage. Stop by for live jazz on Wednesdays.

3 Vintage Lounge
MAP G6 ▪ 1449 W. Taylor St.

The mahogany bar, classic cocktails, and chandeliers at Vintage Lounge will take you back to Old Chicago. A range of pizzas and homemade donuts are on the menu.

4 Punch House
MAP B5 ▪ 1227 W. 18th St.

Hidden away in the basement of Dusek's restaurant, Punch House looks like a swinging 1970s recreation room. Potent punches are the specialty of the house.

5 Buddy Guy's Legends
MAP L5 ▪ 700 S. Wabash Ave.

Run by bluesman Buddy Guy, this club is arguably the city's best. To get a table, come early and dine on decent barbecue food.

Buddy Guy's Legends

6 Jazz Showcase
MAP K5 ▪ 806 S. Plymouth Ct.

Since 1947, this has been Chicago's premiere jazz showroom, hosting the greats past and present. Talkers will be shushed. Sunday afternoon shows are family friendly.

7 Hackney's
MAP K5 ▪ 733 S. Dearborn St.

On Printer's Row, Hackney's offers classic pub grub, including burgers, as well as a good selection of tap beer and a popular patio in season.

8 Cetta's
MAP G6 ▪ 1358 W. Taylor St. ▪ Closed Sun

This dark, intimate Little Italy hideaway is a great place to cozy as a couple before or after dinner with one of forty by-the-glass wines. There is live music on Friday nights.

9 Tufano's Vernon Park Tap
MAP H5 ▪ 1073 W. Vernon Park Pl. ▪ Closed Mon

Also known as Tufano's, this popular bar has legions of local and celebrity fans who pile in for house wine and generous, inexpensive pastas.

10 Hawkeye's Bar & Grill
MAP G6 ▪ 1458 W. Taylor St.

Try this sports bar for beer-fueled camaraderie and a genuine slice of Chicago fan zeal. A shuttle bus even delivers patrons to the United Center and US Cellular Field.

Places to Eat

PRICE CATEGORIES
Price categories include a three-course
meal for one, a glass of house wine, tax,
and a 15–20 percent tip.

$ under $30 $$ $30–$60 $$$ over $60

The informal Eleven City Diner

1 Eleven City Diner
MAP L6 ■ 1112 S. Wabash Ave.
■ 312-212-1112 ■ $

Deli meets diner here, and breakfast
is served all day. Come for sizeable
sandwiches and old-fashioned
fountain drinks such as egg cream.

2 Gioco
MAP K6 ■ 1312 S. Wabash Ave.
■ 312-939-3870 ■ Closed lunch Sat &
Sun ■ $$

Rustic Italian food is the draw at
Gioco, a one-time speakeasy.

3 Pompei Bakery
MAP G6 ■ 1531 W. Taylor St.
■ 312-421-5179 ■ No reservations ■ $

This Little Italy lunch spot showcases
a dozen delicious by-the-slice pizzas.
Hot sandwiches and stuffed pastas
round out the offerings.

4 Acadia
MAP L6 ■ 1639 S. Wabash Ave.
■ 312-360-9500 ■ Closed lunch ■ $$$

Acadia takes its cue from Maine,
offering a fine lobster roll. Tasting
menus come in five and ten courses.

5 Davanti Enoteca
MAP G6 ■ 1359 W. Taylor St. ■
312-226-5550 ■ Closed Mon–Thu ■ $$

A charming wine bar and restaurant
in Little Italy, Davanti Enoteca serves
small plate starters, sharable larger
plates including pastas and pizzas,
and entrées such as grilled swordfish.

6 Chez Joel
MAP H6 ■ 1119 W. Taylor St.
■ 312-226-6479 ■ Closed Mon &
lunch Sun ■ $$

A quaint French bistro in the heart
of Little Italy charms fans with its
sunny decor and fine classics.

7 Francesca's on Taylor
MAP G6 ■ 1400 W. Taylor St. ■
312-829-2828 ■ Closed lunch Sun ■ $

The Little Italy branch of
Wrigleyville's Mia Francesca offers
generous portions of refined Italian
cuisine at reasonable prices.

8 Phoenix
MAP A6 ■ 2131 S. Archer Ave.
■ 312-328-0848 ■ $

Phoenix attracts dim sum diners
from near and far. Go early on
weekends or prepare for long waits.

Diners enjoying dim sum at Phoenix

9 Rosebud Cafe
MAP G6 ■ 1500 W. Taylor St.
■ 312-942-1117 ■ $$

The Italian cooking at Rosebud's,
located in Little Italy, isn't daring but
its convivial vibe is hard to resist.
Long waits for tables are common.

10 Mercat a la Planxa
MAP L5 ■ 638 S. Michigan Ave.
■ 312-765-0524 ■ $$

Arguably the city's best Spanish
restaurant, lively Mercat a la Planxa
specializes in tapas such as bacon-
wrapped dates and juicy lamb chops.
Order suckling pig 72 hours ahead.

See map on pp94–5

TOP 10 Far South

With magnificent architecture, interesting ethnic enclaves, and stand-out museums, Chicago's Far South encompasses districts such as Hyde Park and Kenwood that merit a journey off the beaten tourist path – despite being bordered to the south by some less-than-welcoming neighborhoods.

Hyde Park and Kenwood began life as suburbs for the wealthy escaping the dirty city; today, this part of town is a fascinating melting pot of University of Chicago students and Mexican, Asian, African-American, and Indian residents. Recreation and leisure opportunities abound on spectacular tracts of green space, including the University of Chicago's Midway Plaisance and Jackson Park, site of the 1893 World's Columbian Exposition *(see p23)*.

Detail of a relief, Oriental Institute

AREA MAP OF FAR SOUTH

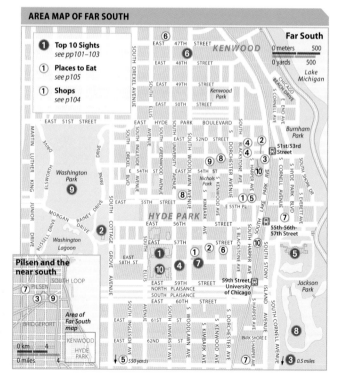

- **1** Top 10 Sights
  see pp101–103
- **1** Places to Eat
  see p105
- **1** Shops
  see p104

University of Chicago campus

① University of Chicago
MAP E6 ▪ 5801 S. Ellis Ave. ▪ Metra station: 55th St. ▪ 1-773-702-1234 ▪ www.uchicago.edu

Noted for its research and high educational standards, this remarkable private university has produced over 80 Nobel Prize winning alumni and staff *(see p50)*.

② DuSable Museum of African American History
MAP D5 ▪ 740 E. 56th Pl. ▪ Open 10am–5pm Tue–Sat, noon–5pm Sun ▪ Adm (free Sun) ▪ DA ▪ www.dusablemuseum.org

Located on the eastern edge of Washington Park, this museum is named after Chicago's first non-native settler, Jean Baptiste Point du Sable. The permanent exhibits celebrate other firsts, such as the first black US astronaut, Major Robert Lawrence, and Chicago's first African-American mayor, Harold Washington. Thought-provoking exhibits include rusted slave shackles and the "Freedom Now" mural, depicting 400 years of African-American history from the early days of slavery to Civil Rights marches.

③ Stony Island Arts Bank
MAP F6 ▪ 6760 S. Stony Island Ave. ▪ 312-857-5561 ▪ Open 11am–6pm Tue–Sat ▪ DA

In 2015, contemporary artist Theaster Gates, Jr. converted this once-grand 1893 bank into an exhibition and arts space, fostering gentrification in a region much in need of investment. The center houses the record collection of the late Chicago DJ Frankie Knuckles, considered the father of House music, and over 60,000 glass lantern slides from the art history department at the University of Chicago. Both collections can be visited during free hour-long tours offered every Saturday at 1pm.

Exhibits at the DuSable Museum

4 Oriental Institute

MAP E6 ▪ 1155 E. 58th St.
▪ 10am–5pm Tue & Thu–Sun (to 8pm
Wed) ▪ DA ▪ www.oi.uchicago.edu

Learn about the origins of agriculture, the invention of writing, the birth of civilization, and the beginning of the study of arts, science, politics, and religion at this University of Chicago museum. Five galleries showcase ancient Near Eastern civilizations from about 3500 BC to AD 100; most exhibits were unearthed during the department's own excavations.

Museum of Science and Industry

5 Museum of Science and Industry

The largest science museum within a single building in the Western Hemisphere, this popular museum attracts over two million people a year (see pp20–21).

6 Kenwood Historic District

MAP E5 ▪ Boundaries: E. 43rd St. (north), E. 51st St. (south), S. Blackstone Ave. (east), and S. Drexel Blvd. (west)

This wealthy enclave within Kenwood, founded by John A. Kennicott in 1856, has mansions that must be seen to be believed. In the late 19th century this area was an upscale Chicago suburb, where wealthy residents built majestic homes on spacious lots, a rarity in the quickly booming city. A stroll around the district uncovers architectural styles ranging from Italianate and Colonial Revival to Prairie style, by influential figures such as Howard Van Doren Shaw and Frank Lloyd Wright (see pp36–7).

7 Robie House

MAP E6 ▪ 5757 S. Woodlawn Ave. ▪ Tour times and prices vary; for information and to buy tickets, call 312-994-4000 or visit www.gowright. org ▪ No DA

This splendid 1910 residence by Frank Lloyd Wright is easily spotted by its steel-beam roof, which overhangs the building by 20 ft (6 m) at each end. Take a tour through its low-ceilinged interior, past more than 170 art-glass windows and doors, to gain insight into the ten-year restoration program. The building was a private home until 1926, when it became a dormitory for the Chicago Theological Seminary. It was later bought by a development firm, who donated it to the University of Chicago in 1963, the same year it was designated a National Historic Landmark.

8 Osaka Japanese Gardens

MAP F6 ▪ Jackson Park, 58th St. & Lake Shore Dr. ▪ Open dawn–dusk ▪ DA

At the north end of Jackson Park's serene Wooded Island (excellent for bird-watching) lies this hushed retreat, complete with meandering paths, lagoons, and fountains. The garden is a partial re-creation of the one formed in 1934 around the beautiful Japanese Pavilion built for the 1893 Expo, which sadly burned down in 1946. The gardens were renamed in 1993 for one of Chicago's sister cities, Osaka, which donated the Japanese gate seen here.

Decorative bridges cross the lagoon, Os

9 Washington Park

MAP D5 ■ Open dawn–11pm (approx) ■ DA

Frederick Law Olmsted and Calvert Vaux, the designers of New York's Central Park, also created this 371-acre green space in the early 1870s. It originally attracted mainly wealthy city dwellers but today, it is a widely used park with recreational programs, the DuSable Museum of African American History, and Lorado Taft's 110-ft (34-m) long sculpture, *Fountain of Time*, which took him 14 years to build. It is unwise to venture into the park after dark.

Lorado Taft's sculpture, Washington Park

10 University of Chicago Sculptures

Over the years, the University of Chicago has acquired around 12 outdoor sculptures, including Wolf Vostell's playful 1970 *Concrete Traffic*, a car embedded in concrete at the southwest end of Midway Plaisance, and *Nuclear Energy*, a bronze by Henry Moore that resembles a mushroom cloud. Within a reflecting pool at 60th Street and University Avenue is *Construction in Space in the Third and Fourth Dimension*, an abstract piece created in the 1950s by Constructivist Antoine Pevsner, which depicts the space-time continuum.

...anese Gardens

EXPLORING FAR SOUTH

▶ MORNING

Start your day with a true South Side classic, the cafeteria **Valois** *(see p105)*, which draws everyone from local pensioners to former President Obama. From there, walk about a mile (1.6 km) south or hop on the no. 28 bus at the corner of Hyde Park Boulevard and Lake Park Avenue to visit the **Museum of Science and Industry** *(see pp20–21)*, where you can easily spend an engrossing few hours exploring the hands-on exhibits. For lunch, skip the museum food and head west about a mile (1.6 km) to **Medici on 57th** *(see p105)*, a great student and faculty hangout, known for its delicious pizzas. The extravagant Garbage Pizza is a favorite.

AFTERNOON

Stroll about four blocks southwest to the **Oriental Institute** at the **University of Chicago** *(see p101)* whose museum will transport you back to ancient times. Its Suq gift shop offers unique souvenirs, such as a replica of an ancient board game. Just east of the institute is Frank Lloyd Wright's masterpiece of Prairie-style architecture, **Robie House**. Take a tour of this to really gain some insight into the great man's vision. Then stroll around the university's leafy quadrangles if it's good weather, or backtrack a little to the **Smart Museum of Art** *(see p50)* if you'd rather be inside. Either way, round off your day with a culinary trip to the French-Italian border at **A10** *(see p105)*.

See map on p100 ←

Shops

Shelves stacked high, Seminary Co-op Bookstore

1 Seminary Co-op Bookstore

MAP E6 ▪ 5751 S. Woodlawn Ave.

Housed in the basement of the Chicago Theological Seminary on the University of Chicago campus, this bookstore has a well-respected academic section, especially humanities and social sciences.

2 57th Street Books

MAP E6 ▪ 1301 E. 57th St.
▪ No DA

This basement-level shop carries new fiction, children's books, and African-American interest titles. Low ceilings, brick walls, and a painted cement floor all create a cozy atmosphere, conducive to browsing.

3 Modern Cooperative

MAP B5 ▪ 1215 W. 18th St.

Specializing in restored mid-20th-century modern furniture, this destination boutique was born of its owners' love for searching the open road for rare bargains. It also has contemporary interpretations of classic styles.

4 Alise's Designer Shoes

MAP F5 ▪ 5210C S. Harper Ave.

Shop for the latest designer shoe fashions from Italy, France, Brazil, and the Far East, as well as ladies' bags, fine jewelry, and men's belts.

5 Toys et Cetera

MAP F5 ▪ 5211 S. Harper Ave.

This inviting store focuses on good old-fashioned toys galore. Classic standbys include kites, face-painting kits, balls, and dress-up clothes.

6 Little Black Pearl Workshop

MAP C6 ▪ 1060 E. 47th St.
▪ Closed Sun

The gift shop at this cultural arts center sells the students' creations, such as one-of-a-kind painted furniture and vibrant mosaics.

7 House of Africa

MAP F6 ▪ 1510 E. 63rd St.
▪ Closed Sun

The scent of sandlewood incense fills this small boutique that sells African artifacts, carved wooden sculptures, and CDs of music from all over the continent.

8 Hyde Park Records

MAP E5 ▪ 1377 E. 53rd St.

This is the place to start up, or fill the gaps in, your record collection, with reasonable prices and friendly, knowledgable staff. New and used vinyl and CDs cover a wide range of genres, and there are some excellent bargains to be had.

9 Kilimanjaro International

MAP E5 ▪ 1305 E. 53rd St.

Reflecting the surrounding community's African roots, this fine arts and crafts specialty store features everything from hand-crafted jewelry to ceremonial masks.

10 Powell's Bookstore

MAP E6 ▪ 1501 E. 57th St.

Here, used books in top condition are stacked floor to ceiling on painted wood shelves, with antique editions protected behind glass.

Places to Eat

PRICE CATEGORIES
Price categories include a three-course meal for one, a glass of house wine, tax, and a 15–20 percent tip.

$ under $30 $$ $30–$60 $$$ over 60

1 La Petite Folie
MAP E5 ▪ 1504 E. 55th St. ▪ 1-773-493-1394 ▪ Closed Mon, Sat & Sun lunch ▪ $$

An upscale French restaurant offering a fixed-price menu, as well as entrées featuring ingredients such as rabbit and quail.

2 Valois
MAP F5 ▪ 1518 E. 53rd St. ▪ 1-773-667-0647 ▪ $

The cafeteria that proudly demands that you "see your food," Valois offers stick-to-your ribs comfort food, from roast beef to goulash. Cash only.

3 The Promontory
MAP F5 ▪ 5311 S. Lake Park Ave. ▪ 312-801-2100 ▪ Open 5:30am–10pm daily ▪ $$

With a menu spanning snacks and mains, the savory Southern food has a farm-to-table focus. There is live and DJ-spun music on most nights.

Outside terrace, The Promontory

4 A10
MAP F5 ▪ 1462 E. 53rd St ▪ 1-773-288-1010 ▪ Closed lunch ▪ $$
The menu at A10 takes its inspiration from the French and Italian rivieras.

5 Harold's Chicken Shack
MAP C5 ▪ 2109 S. Wabash Ave. ▪ 312-326-5575 ▪ $

Enjoy fast soul food, including catfish and fried chicken at this casual, authentic café.

6 Medici on 57th
MAP E6 ▪ 1327 E. 57th St. ▪ 1-773-667-7394 ▪ $$

Great pizzas draw the crowds here, but sandwiches on home-baked bread and rich milkshakes are also offered. Guests are welcome to bring their own beer or wine to accompany their meal.

7 Lagunitas Brewery Company
MAP B5 ▪ 1843 S. Washtenaw Ave. ▪ 1-707-769-4495 ▪ Open noon–9pm Wed–Sun ▪ $

At its massive brewery, Lagunitas has set up a taproom featuring fresh beer as well as live music and a beer-friendly menu with dishes such as pulled-pork nachos.

8 Woodlawn Tap
MAP E5 ▪ 1172 E. 55th St. ▪ 1-773-643-5516 ▪ $

A casual dress code, good food, and cheap beer attract all types to this bar, especially for the tasty burgers and hearty soup.

9 Dusek's Board and Beer
MAP B5 ▪ 1227 W. 18th St. ▪ 312-526-3851 ▪ $$

In offbeat historic surroundings, Dusek's serves an upscale menu with tap beer pairings. Upstairs, Thalia Hall stages concerts under a separate admission.

10 Chant
MAP E5 ▪ 1509 E. 53rd St. ▪ 1-773-324-1999 ▪ $

With its funky vibe, unique cocktails, and global fusion cuisine, Chant is great at any time, but its Sunday brunch with live music is particularly good – and a real bargain.

See map on p100

Streetsmart

The elevated "L" train threading its way through the skyscrapers

Getting To and Around Chicago

Arriving by Air

Most international and many domestic flights arrive at **O'Hare International Airport**, one of the world's busiest airports, located 20 miles (32 km) northwest of downtown Chicago. Serving most major airlines, including most international flights, this big and sprawling airport offers free transportation between its four terminals via the Airport Transport System (ATS) train.

The Chicago Transit Authority's Blue Line "L" train connects O'Hare to downtown; follow airport signs that say "Trains to City." Trips take about 30 minutes. Taxis are available from the lower arrivals level of each terminal. When the roads are clear it can take 40 minutes to reach downtown, but time can quickly double with traffic.

Car rental agencies are located near the baggage claim areas in terminals 1–3, and via courtesy telephones from terminal 5 (do not be confused by the numbering; there is no terminal 4 at O'Hare).

Midway International Airport is Chicago's second airport. Located 10 miles (16 km) southwest of downtown, it serves mostly domestic airlines, including several popular budget carriers such as Southwest Airlines. Taxis are available from the lower arrivals level; car rental agencies are located in the main terminal building; and shuttle buses leave from in front of it. The CTA's Orange Line "L" connects Midway and downtown in trips of less than 30 minutes.

Available near baggage reclaim at both airports, **GO Airport Express** will drop off (and pick up) at any requested downtown location; book the return airport shuttle in advance. Several companies, including **Elite Chicago Limo**, offer private door-to-door services booked in advance at rates that are higher than taxis.

Arriving by Train

Up to 56 **Amtrak** trains serve Union Station in downtown each day, ranging from cross-country routes to a commuter service to nearby Milwaukee. The nearest "L" stop to Union station is at Clinton, but it's a good walk, so it is often better to take a cab or bus to your destination.

Arriving by Road

The inexpensive **Megabus** links Chicago with lots of other Midwestern cities, and the bus stop is directly opposite Union Station. Tickets must be booked online and are not sold by the driver or on the bus. **Greyhound** buses offer service throughout the country from its terminal in the South Loop, where travelers can walk up and buy tickets.

Those arriving by car generally do so via the busy Interstate highways, including I-55 from the southwest, I-57 from the south, I-88 from the west, I-90 from the east and northwest, and I-94 from the east and north. Route 66 from Santa Monica, CA joins I-55 before hitting downtown Chicago.

Getting Around by Train

Short for elevated train, the "L" is nevertheless the name given to the entire **Chicago Transit Authority** (CTA) train network, including the sections that travel underground. The eight lines are identifiable by color: red, green, blue, brown, orange, pink, purple, and yellow. The red and blue lines run 24 hours a day (less often off-peak). Trains arrive every 5 to 20 minutes, and the service is fast and economical. Its smartphone app provides real-time schedules.

Metra, the commuter rail system, serves the city's suburbs. Downtown stops are Union Station, LaSalle Street Station, Ogilvie Transportation Center, and Randolph Street Station.

By Bus

The CTA bus network covers the entire city and the suburbs, and is especially useful for reaching the lakefront, which is not served by the "L". Keep an eye out for the blue and white bus stop signs.

PACE buses also service the city suburbs and are numbered 208 and higher.

Tickets

The regular "L" or bus fare is $2.25, with an extra 25¢ for a transfer card (valid for two transfers within two hours of purchase), and you need exact change. You can buy a Ventra transit card with a preset value or a top-up Transit card and charge it with the desired amount at an automated vending machine at any station. The relevant fare is then deducted from your pass each time you take a ride. You can buy 1- to 7-day CTA Passes from over 1,000 retail locations including drug stores and Currency Exchanges.

Metra fares vary according to the journey's length. Tickets may be purchased at automated kiosks at each station.

By Taxi

It is usually easy to hail a cab downtown and in popular neighborhoods in commercial areas; in residential districts, it's better to call for one. There's an initial charge, then a fee per mile and per extra passenger. A 10–15 percent tip is expected. Companies include: **Checker Taxi Assoc.**, **Flash Cab Co.**, and **Yellow Cab Co.** The ride-sharing service **Uber** is also popular, summoning a driver using their personal car. Users can only access Uber drivers using the smartphone app.

May through September, **Chicago Water Taxi** runs boats between the Wrigley Building and a stop for both Union Station and the Ogilvie Transportation Center. **Shoreline Water Taxis** also offer a frequent service on the Chicago River to Willis Tower as well as on Lake Michigan from Navy Pier to the John G. Shedd Aquarium.

By Car

Driving in the city is not recommended. Parking is difficult to find and often expensive, and heavy traffic is common. Those arriving by car are advised to leave their vehicle in a parking lot and use public transportation or taxis to get around. However, for those who would like to get beyond the metropolitan area, the car-share service **Zipcar** offers rentals by the hour or by the day. Members should apply online prior to reserving a car; charges include gas and insurance.

By Bicycle

Chicago has more than 200 miles (322 km) of bike lanes on its city streets, and encourages short commutes via cycle with its bike-share service, **Divvy**. Riders can purchase a 24-hour pass for $9.95 at any of the hundreds of Divvy bike stations around the 18 miles (29 km) of lakefront bike paths.

On Foot

The best way to explore Chicago, particularly downtown and Northside areas (including the Mag Mile and Lincoln Park), is by walking. Avoid south of the South Loop after dark.

Practical Information

Passports and Visas

Citizens of EU countries, Australia, Chile, Iceland, New Zealand, and Japan can spend up to 90 days in the US without a visa, so long as they have a valid passport and a round-trip ticket. They will also need to register with the **US Department of Homeland Security** and pay a fee online prior to departure. Canadian citizens must show a valid passport. Citizens of other countries should contact their local US embassy well in advance of their trip to obtain the relevant visa.

Customs and Immigration

Landing cards and customs forms are distributed on the plane. Often travelers will also be required to enter such information on a computer screen in the entry hall. Foreign nationals have to join a separate line to have these and their passports inspected after landing. Strict security checks, involving the taking of photographs and fingerprints, are now in place for those arriving in the US on a visa. Note that any person entering the US is required to stay off their cell phones while in the immigration line.

US Customs and Border Protection stipulates that visitors can bring up to $100 of merchandize as gifts per family duty-free. The $100 cap may include 100 cigars but no alcohol.

Travel Safety Advice

Visitors can get up-to-date travel safety information from the **Foreign and Commonwealth Office** in the UK, the **State Department** in the US, and the **Department of Foreign Affairs and Trade** in Australia.

Travel Insurance

A comprehensive travel insurance policy is recommended. This should include cover for trip cancellation, lost luggage, car rental insurance and medical expenses, which are high in America.

Rental car agencies offer vehicle coverage (which can be high), but many credit cards, home owner's insurance policies, and banks extend vehicle coverage. Check with your credit card, insurer or bank before leaving home.

Emergency Services

For police, fire, and medical emergencies, dial 911. If you are not in a position to speak, the emergency locator should still be able to track you. For non-emergency police matters, such as theft or vandalism, dial 311 to reach the City Helpline. Both numbers can be accessed by cell phones.

Health

Tap water is potable and special vaccinations are not required. Carry with you prescriptions for medications that you take. For serious illnesses, see the hospitals and emergency rooms listed in the Yellow Pages of the telephone directory. **Weiss Memorial Hospital** and **Northwestern Memorial Hospital** are convenient to downtown and the city's Northside, while **Bernard A. Mitchell Hospital**, at the University of Chicago, serves the South Side.

Even with medical insurance, you may have to pay for services and claim reimbursement after. Contact your insurer before receiving any treatment. Many dental clinics are open 24 hours and available for emergency procedures. Check with the hotel concierge or contact the **Chicago Dental Society** for a referral.

Pharmacies are plentiful throughout the city. Many drug stores are open 24 hours. The most popular drug store chains, including **Walgreens** and **CVS**, all have pharmacies inside. The pharmacies, however, even in 24-hour drug stores, are often only open during regular business hours and often close on Sunday.

Chicago is a city of extreme seasons. Visitors should be prepared for cold, windy, and snowy winters, which can create hazardous conditions. A hat, gloves, and suitable footwear are essential. In summer, the extreme heat can also cause health problems: ensure you apply sunscreen, wear a hat, and drink plenty of water.

Personal Security

As in most cities, the most common crimes are pickpocketing and purse snatching. Common sense can help deter these problems. Leave surplus cash, credit cards, and valuables in a safe place at your hotel, preferably a locked safe in the room. Don't walk around with your wallet in a back pocket, and keep bags securely fastened and close to your body. Keep a copy of your credit card numbers (and the number to call if they are lost) separate from the cards, and bring with you photocopies of important documents, including passports, in case they are stolen.

It's best to avoid using public transportation very late at night. Take a taxi instead. Train platforms and trains usually have an intercom in case of emergency. At night, avoid walking alone in dimly lit areas and in parks. Steer clear of areas on the far West Side of the city and parts of the South Side where crime levels are much higher.

Currency and Banking

The US currency is the dollar ($), which is divided into 100 cents. Paper notes are in denominations of $1, $5, $10, $20, $50, and $100. Coins are 50 cents, 25 cents, 10 cents, 5 cents, and 1 penny. Coins valued at $1 and $2 are in circulation, but are very rarely used.

ATMs (cash machines) abound and are the easiest way to get money, though most banks charge a fee for use and another for the exchange rate. The machines will list the fees and ask you if you wish to accept them before continuing with the transaction.

Banks tend to offer better exchange rates than the exchange windows found at the airports, though rates vary from bank to bank and not all banks offer foreign exchanges.

As an emergency stash, US dollar traveler's checks can be changed at most banks and foreign exchanges by showing a photo ID. They can also normally be used in stores and restaurants.

Credit cards are widely accepted and commonly used, even for small purchases like a coffee. Some smaller, family-run establishments only accept cash, but those with this policy usually advertise this clearly, often with signs in their windows.

DIRECTORY

PASSPORTS AND VISAS

US Department of Homeland Security
w esta.cbp.dhs.gov

EMBASSIES AND CONSULATES

Australia
MAP J4 ■ 123 N. Wacker Dr. ☎ 312-419-1480
w usa.embassy.gov.au

Canada
MAP L4 ■ 180 N. Stetson Ave.
☎ 312-616-1860
w chicago.gc.ca

Ireland
MAP K3 ■ 1 E. Wacker Dr.
☎ 312-337-2700
w irishconsulate.org

New Zealand
w nzembassy.com

UK
MAP L3 ■ 625 N. Michigan Ave.
☎ 312-970-3800
w gov.uk

CUSTOMS AND IMMIGRATION

US Customs and Border Protection
w cbp.gov

TRAVEL SAFETY ADVICE

Department of Foreign Affairs and Trade
w dfat-gov-au
w smartraveller.gov.au

Foreign and Commonwealth Office
w gov.uk/foreign-travel-advice

US State Department
w travel.state.gov

HEALTH

Bernard A. Mitchell Hospital
MAP E6 ■ 5841 S. Maryland Ave.
☎ 1-773-702-1000
w uchospitals.edu

Chicago Dental Society
☎ 312-836-7300
w cds.org

CVS
w cvs.com

Northwestern Memorial Hospital
MAP L2 ■ 201 E. Huron St.
☎ 312-926-3627
w nm.org

Walgreens
w walgreens.com

Weiss Memorial Hospital
4646 N. Marine Dr.
☎ 1-773-878-8700
w weisshospital.com

Internet and Telephone

Many cafes and hotels offer free Wi-Fi, usually accessible by a password available for the asking. The City of Chicago offers free public Wi-Fi in hotspots around the city, including all 79 Chicago Public Library locations, the Cultural Center (see p71), Daley Plaza (see p75), and Millennium Park (see pp34–5).

Chicago has two area codes: 312 for downtown and the immediate vicinity; 773 for the rest of the city, including the Northside and South Side. Dial 1 + the area code for any US number outside the area code you are in; cell phones do not require a 1 before the full number, including the area code. To dial abroad, key in 011 + country code + city code (omitting any initial 0).

Public phones, which accept both coins and credit cards, are fast disappearing in the wake of cell phone ubiquity. Most mobile phones work in America if unlocked by your carrier. Check the costs and data packages available before you travel, or consider buying a local SIM card to avoid high roaming charges.

Postal Services

Most branches of the **US Postal Service** are open 9am–6pm Monday to Friday and 9am–1pm Saturday. Some neighbourhood locations may have more abbreviated hours, and others may also be open for a few hours on Sunday morning. Many stores, including grocery stores and drug stores, sell stamps. Mailboxes are navy blue and posted on many street corners.

Television and Radio

For local TV, there's a wide range to choose from: CBS (Channel 2); NBC (Channel 5); ABC (Channel 7); WGN (Channel 9); WTTW Public TV (Channel 11); and Fox (Channel 32). Most TVs also offer a wide range of cable TV programming.

The most popular radio stations include: WFMT (98.7 FM) for classical, WLUP (97.9 FM) for rock, WGCI (107.5 FM) for R&B, and WXRT (93.1 FM) for adult alternative. WBBM (780 AM) is a news station, as is Chicago Public Radio WBEZ (91.5 FM), and WSCR (670 AM) covers sports.

Newspapers and Magazines

The city's two main daily newspapers are the *Chicago Tribune* and the *Chicago Sun-Times*. Both are widely available, and also offer their news stories online. The free alternative weekly *The Reader* offers local arts, dining and theater reviews plus lifestyle and political stories, as does the monthly magazine *Chicago Magazine*. The online-only magazine *Time Out Chicago* offers good suggestions for entertainment and dining.

Opening Hours

Office hours for businesses are generally 9am–5pm Monday to Friday. Shop and mall hours can vary but they are usually open 10am–9pm Monday to Saturday and noon–5pm Sunday. However, Northside boutiques and stores along the Mag Mile often stay open until 7 or 8pm nightly, except on Sunday.

Banks are usually open during regular office hours only, which is normally 9am–5pm Monday to Friday, though most banks offer 24-hour access to ATM machines, many times in indoor halls that require you to swipe your bank card to gain admission.

Museums and attractions keep their own various hours, though many extend their hours during the summer season and some offer at least one evening with extended opening hours each week. It is best to consult their websites before going to avoid disappointment.

Most banks, shops, offices, and attractions are closed over public holidays including New Year's Day (Jan 1); Martin Luther King Day (3rd Mon in Jan); President's Day (3rd Mon in Feb); Casimir Pulaski Day (1st Mon in Mar); Memorial Day (last Mon in May); Independence Day (July 4); Labor Day (1st Mon in Sep); Thanksgiving (4th Thu in Nov); and Christmas Day (Dec 25).

Time Difference

Chicago operates on Central Time (6 hours behind GMT). Daylight savings time begins at 3am on the first Sunday in April, when the clocks are moved forward an hour, and reverts to standard time at 1am on the last Sunday in October when they are then moved back an hour.

Electrical Appliances

Electrical appliances in the US operate on 110–120 volts and use two-prong plugs. Non-US, single-voltage appliances need a transformer and an adapter, commonly available in airport shops, electrical stores, and large department stores.

Driving Licenses

Foreign or out-of-state driver's licenses are valid in Chicago – if they are in English. Bring your picture license even if you don't plan to rent a car: it's a good alternative to a passport if you are asked for proof of age in a bar.

Weather

Chicago winters are usually intemperate, with frequent heavy snow and temperatures ranging from 13° F (-9° C) to 37° F (4° C). Summer days can be anything from balmy to boiling, averaging 69° F (22° C) to 84° F (30° C). Extremes, like winter blizzards, heavy spring rains, and summer heat waves are not uncommon, with spring-time weather being particularly changeable. Despite the winds that can gust off Lake Michigan, Chicago's "Windy City" moniker is actually attributed to the verbose bid the city made to host the 1893 World's Columbian Exposition.

When to Go

For a moderate climate, the best time to visit Chicago is spring or fall. But if you can bear the bitter cold of the festive season you'll see the city sparkle with Christmas lights – and you'll have a lot fewer tourists to contend with. Summer sees street festivities and live music in the parks. Try to avoid visiting in November, when hotels are full of conventioneers.

Travelers with Special Needs

The majority of hotels restaurants, shops, malls, and museums are accessible to wheelchair users. Many sidewalks offer curb cuts that allow smooth passage when crossing the streets. Most buses and train stations are also wheelchair accessible. The non-profit **Open Doors Organization** runs a website with information for travelers with disabilities. The **Mayor's Office for People with Disabilities** offers information on disabled access around town.

Sources of Information

Chicago has two main tourist information centers: located in the Chicago Cultural Center (see p71) and in Macy's department store (see p76) in the Loop. Opening hours are at least 10am–5pm Monday to Saturday and 11am–4pm Sunday (the Macy's location keeps depart-ment store hours). You can also get further

(see p71)
(see p76)

DIRECTORY

POSTAL SERVICES

US Postal Service
w usps.com

NEWSPAPERS AND MAGAZINES

Chicago Magazine
w chicagomag.com

Chicago Sun-Times
w chicago.suntimes. com

Chicago Tribune
w chicagotribune.com

The Reader
w chicagoreader.com

Time Out Chicago
w timeout.com/chicago

TRAVELERS WITH SPECIAL NEEDS

Mayor's Office for People with Disabilities
w cityofchicago.org

Open Doors Organization
w easyaccesschicago. org

SOURCES OF INFORMATION

Choose Chicago
w choosechicago.com

Eater Chicago
w chicago.eater.com

MetroMix
w metromix.com

Theatre in Chicago
w theatreinchicago.com

information at the city's official tourism website **Choose Chicago**, which is updated regularly. For in-depth reviews of where to go and what to see, log onto **MetroMix**, affiliated to the *Chicago Tribune*. The popular web site **Eater Chicago** offers comprehensive dining information. **Theatre in Chicago**, also online, offers up-to-date information on shows around town.

Trips and Tours

Run by Choose Chicago, the free **Chicago Greeters** service gives you a chance to spend 2 to 4 hours with enthusiastic locals who love the city (book online 10 days in advance). For more spontaneous tours, **InstaGreeters** are available for hour-long tours Friday to Sunday.

For design buffs, the **Chicago Architectural Foundation** tours offer itineraries focused on the city's architecture by walking, bike, bus, or (in summer) boat tour. The trips highlight both historic and modern buildings, including Frank Lloyd Wright's architectural legacy. They also run occasional Loop Train Tours – a great opportunity to glimpse ornate facades that are often invisible from the sidewalks below.

Delve into some of the city's infamous 1920s and 1930s gangster residents with **Untouchable Tours**. On board a custom-built bus, sites visited on this 2-hour tour include that of the St. Valentine's Day Massacre, Little Italy.

Many boat companies, including **Wendella** and **Shoreline Sightseeing**, offer ways to see the city from the river and the lake. Leaving from Navy Pier, **Seadog Cruises** provide tours of both in fast speedboats. Enjoy a meal or cocktails and dancing onboard the elegant *Odyssey* or *Spirit of Chicago* mega-yachts, also moored at Navy Pier. In summer, the four-masted schooner *Windy*, also sails the lake.

More active options for exploring include tours from **Bike & Roll Chicago**. Cycling tours will guide you through the city's parks, neighborhoods, or along the lakefront. Themed departures include yoga and biking, brewery by bike, and food tours. The company also offers itineraries via Segways. **Bobby's Bike Hike** also offers themed cycling tours.

Paddle down the Chicago River while learning about the city's history with **Wateriders**; they offer gangster- and ghost-themed tours for both beginners and advanced paddlers.

Shopping

Chicago is a great shopping destination, combining all the major brands and designers with neighborhood boutiques and interesting art and craft galleries.

You're in shopper's heaven when it comes to department stores, which are mostly located on North Michigan Avenue and State Street. They include traditional **Macy's**, upscale **Nordstrom**, and stylish **Bloomingdale's**.

There's no shortage of malls in the city, especially vertical ones on the Mag Mile. Here you'll find **Water Tower Place**, **Westfield North Bridge**, and **900 North Michigan Shops**. Among discount stores, look for bargains at **Nordstrom Rack** in two downtown locations.

Authentic local food, such as pizza and Eli's cheesecake, can be shipped anywhere in the US by **Taste of Chicago**.

Many Chicago stores have items on sale all year round, but expect real bargains after Christmas, on Presidents' Day (third Monday in February), and on Labor Day (first Monday in September).

Chicago state and local sales taxes are among the highest in the country at 10.25 percent on all non-food items.

Clothing and shoe sizes in the UK, Europe, and the US differ. Look at www.onlineconversion.com for help with sizes.

Where to Eat

Chicago is considered one of the country's dining meccas, with specialties at both the high and low ends of the scale, including acclaimed chef-run restaurants and beefy steakhouses down to popular hot dog and taco stands. The city is best known for its deep-dish pizza, which is highly filling, caloric, and fun.

Restaurant styles run the gamut from gourmet to casual, and many neighborhoods are hives of ethnic cuisine. Most chef-run places will accommodate dietary restrictions, and many restaurants label dishes if they are vegan, vegetarian, low-calorie or gluten-free.

Most restaurants take reservations and many require advance booking on weekends. The free restaurant reservation site **Open Table** is a good source for one-click tables.

With the exception of very high-end places, most restaurants are family friendly, offering kids' menus, high chairs, and even crayons.

This is especially true at neighborhood restaurants, though hotel eateries are also very accommodating.

Breakfast is usually served in diners and coffee shops from about 6am to 10am. Lunch is normally available from 11:30am to 2pm, and dinner takes place from approximately 5 to 10pm, depending on the spot.

Tipping is expected for waiters at 15–20 percent of the bill before taxes. Taxes will add 10.7 percent to your food bill.

Where to Stay

Chicago offers every kind of accommodation possible, from a berth on a boat to a luxury hotel. The former and other unusual options, as well as a room in someone's home, can be found at **Airbnb**. The popular home-sharing service can often source entire apartments at bargain rates.

Most accommodations are in hotels, which vary from big convention-focused options to small and stylish boutiques. The best in terms of location are downtown.

Hotel rates vary according to the hotel category, and the time of week and season. Peak rates are from April to December and often coincide with business travel traffic in town. This means weekends can be a good time to save, though summer rates are highest no matter what day of the week. Rack rates (the basic room rates) are the ones used in this book to provide a guide price. It is almost always possible to get a better deal, so don't be too shy to ask. Usually, the larger the room, the higher the tab, and many, though not all, hotels charge more for a room with a view – so consider how much time you will want to spend in your room before you pay the premium. Twin-bedded rooms are uncommon; most double rooms have either a queen- or king-sized bed or two double beds. Rates are subject to a 17.4 percent hotel tax. For hotel deals, see **Hotel Tonight** or **Booking.com.**

The selection of B&Bs, listed at the **Chicago Bed and Breakfast Association (CBBA)**, are a great way to see the city from a new perspective.

DIRECTORY

TRIPS AND TOURS

Bike & Roll Chicago
w bikechicago.com

Bobby's Bike Hike
w bobbysbikehike.com

Chicago Architectural Foundation
w architecture.org

Chicago Greeters and InstaGreeters
w chicagogreeter.com

Odyssey
w odysseycruises.com

Seadog Cruises
w seadogcruises.com

Shoreline Sightseeing
w shorelinesightseeing.com

Spirit of Chicago
w spiritcruises.com

Untouchable Tours
w gangstertour.com

Wateriders
w wateriders.com

Wendella
w wendellaboats.com

Windy
w tallshipwindy.com

SHOPPING

900 North Michigan Shops
MAP L2 ▪ 900 N. Michigan Ave.
w shop900.com

Bloomingdale's
MAP L2 ▪ 900 N. Michigan Ave.
w bloomingdales.com

Macy's
MAP K4 ▪ 111 N. State St.
w macys.com

Nordstrom
MAP L3 ▪ 520 N. Michigan Ave.
w nordstrom.com

Nordstrom Rack
MAP K4 ▪ 24 N. State St. and 101 E. Chicago Ave.
w nordstromrack.com

Tastes of Chicago
w tastesofchicago.com

Water Tower Place
MAP L2 ▪ 835 N. Michigan Ave.
w shopwatertower.com

Westfield North Bridge
MAP L3 ▪ 520 N. Michigan Ave.
w theshopsatnorthbridge.com

WHERE TO EAT

Open Table
w opentable.com

WHERE TO STAY

Airbnb
w airbnb.com

Booking.com
w booking.com

CBBA
w chicago-bed-breakfast.com

Hotel Tonight
w hoteltonight.com

Places to Stay

PRICE CATEGORIES
For a standard, double room per night (with breakfast if included), taxes and extra charges.
....
$ under $200 **$$** $200–$400 **$$$** over $400

Luxury Hotels

The Gwen
MAP L3 ▪ 521 N. Rush St. ▪ 312-645-1500 ▪ www.thegwenchicago.com ▪ $$
Tucked discreetly above the Shops at North Bridge on the Magnificent Mile, the 300-room Gwen, lodged in the historic 1929 McGraw-Hill Building, takes its name from sculptress Gwen Lux whose relief panels adorn the hotel. Its fifth-floor terrace bar is a haven on the teeming street.

InterContinental Chicago
MAP L2 ▪ 505 N. Michigan Ave. ▪ 312-944-4100 ▪ www.icchicago.com ▪ $$
This former men's club (see p32) has stunning public rooms, including a swimming pool, and very comfortable guest rooms. The mix of historic charm with contemporary elegance makes it one of the city's most luxurious hotels

Trump International Hotel & Tower
MAP K3 ▪ 401 N. Wabash Ave. ▪ 312-588-8000 ▪ www.trumpchicagohotel.com ▪ $$
Chicago's second-highest building (at 92 stories) houses this chic and state-of-the-art hotel. Stylish rooms have electronic amenities and floor-to-ceiling windows with views of Lake Michigan, the Chicago River, and the city skyline.

Four Seasons
MAP L2 ▪ 120 E. Delaware Pl. ▪ 312-280-8800 ▪ www.fourseasons.com ▪ $$$
One can expect the best in this grand hotel – possibly Chicago's most elegant. Lavish rooms command sweeping city and lake views, and the award-winning Seasons restaurant is a must-try.

Langham Chicago
MAP K3 ▪ 330 N. Wabash Ave. ▪ 312-923-9988 ▪ www.langhamhotels.com ▪ $$$
This branch of the Hong Kong-based luxury hotel bridges worldly splendor and mid-century modern Chicago, a cue it takes from its location in a Mies van der Rohe-designed high-rise. The popular second-story bar looks out over the Chicago River and the Chuan Spa offers unusual Asian treatments.

Park Hyatt Chicago
MAP L2 ▪ 800 N. Michigan Ave. ▪ 312-335-1234 ▪ www.parkchicago.hyatt.com ▪ $$$
Original contemporary art, rich woods, and warm tones create comfortable and tranquil public and private areas at this elegant boutique hotel. The state-of-the-art rooms and suites feature furniture designed by Mies van der Rohe. Other facilities include an indoor pool and fitness center.

Peninsula Chicago
MAP L2 ▪ 108 E. Superior St. ▪ 312-337-2888 ▪ www.peninsula.com/chicago ▪ $$$
Understated elegance sums up this hotel, with large, earth-toned rooms that include dressing areas, and a steam-free TV screen and hands-free telephone in every bathroom. Floor-to-ceiling windows dramatize the lobby, where afternoon tea is accompanied by live classical music.

Ritz-Carlton
MAP L2 ▪ 160 E. Pearson St. ▪ 312-266-1000 ▪ www.fourseasons.com ▪ $$$
The Ritz has it all – first-class service, an award-winning dining room, spa, and the best business facilities. Great views complement the classic furniture and fine art in its spacious guest rooms, but it's the little things, like Bulgari toiletries and toys and cookies for the kids, that puts it in a league of its own.

Sofitel Chicago Water Tower
MAP K2 ▪ 20 E. Chestnut St. ▪ 312-324-4000 ▪ www.sofitel.com ▪ $$$
This striking, ultra-modern hotel features spectacular views, sumptuous feather beds, and marble bathrooms in every room. There is also a 24-hour fitness center.

Historic Hotels

Palmer House Hilton
MAP L4 ▪ 17 E. Monroe St.
▪ 312-726-7500 ▪ www.
chicagohilton.com ▪ $
This has been an elegant
fixture in the heart of
the Loop since 1873.
Extravagant frescoes
decorate the ornate
lobby's ceiling, while the
guest rooms are subtly
elegant. The hotel has its
own shopping arcade.

The Tremont
MAP K2 ▪ 100 E. Chestnut
St. ▪ 312-751-1900
▪ www.tremontchicago.
com ▪ $
An inviting fireplace
welcomes you at this
1920s-built hotel, where
guest rooms are small
but comfortable; some
have antique furniture
and four-posters. Mike
Ditka's restaurant is
famous for its steaks
and sports memorabilia.

Chicago Athletic Association
MAP L4 ▪ 12 S. Michigan
Ave. ▪ 312-940-3552
▪ www.chicagoathletic
hotel.com ▪ $$
Originally opened in 1893
as a men's club, the
reincarnation of this
building as a hotel faithfully
restored all the terrazzo
floors, stained glass,
marble staircases, and
other adornments. The
rooftop restaurant and the
vintage-game-filled bar
are among the highlights.

Millennium Knickerbocker
MAP L2 ▪ 163 E. Walton
Pl. ▪ 312-751-8100
▪ www.millennium
hotels.com ▪ $$
This hotel, once owned by
Playboy magazine, has
hosted guests as famous
as John Kennedy and
Al Capone. Its 1930s lobby
holds the Martini Bar (with
live music most days), and
the guest rooms exude a
timeless elegance.

The Talbott
MAP K2 ▪ 20 E. Delaware
Pl. ▪ 312-944-4970
▪ www.talbotthotel.com
▪ $$
Enjoy the quiet elegance
of this small, family-
owned, European-style
hotel. The Victorian
parlor-like lobby and
atmospheric Basil's bar
and café offer a chance to
unwind, and the 149 guest
rooms and suites are
large and welcoming.

Wheeler Mansion
2020 S. Calumet Ave.
▪ 312-945-2020 ▪ www.
wheelermansion.com
▪ $$
An immaculate 11-room
hotel, this mansion dating
to 1870 is known for its
fantastic attention to
detail. Marvel at the
lavish artwork, period
features, and antique
furniture, or relax in the
tranquil garden.

The Whitehall
MAP L2 ▪ 105 E. Delaware
Pl. ▪ 312-944-6300 ▪
www.thewhitehall
hotel.com ▪ $$
A quiet, understated
European ambience has
permeated this hotel
since it opened in 1928.
The 221 guest rooms
combine elegant tradition
with mod cons, and the
Presidential Suite was a
favorite of Katharine
Hepburn. Check out the
Fornetto Mei restaurant
with its menu of neo-
Milanese cuisine and
thin-crust specialty pizzas.

The Drake
MAP L2 ▪ 140 E. Walton
Pl. ▪ 312-787-2200
▪ www.thedrakehotel.
com ▪ $$$
Popular with visiting
celebrities and royalty,
this is the grande dame
of Chicago hotels. A
landmark building on the
the Magnificent Mile, The
Drake effortlessly blends
modern convenience with
the charm of days gone
by. Each of the 535 rooms
and suites is unique, and
many of them offer
breathtaking views.

Hotel Burnham
MAP K4 ▪ 1 W. Washington
St. ▪ 312-782-1111
▪ www.burnhamhotel.
com ▪ $$$
The Reliance Building
(see p42) – a handsome
example of the Chicago
school of architecture –
was reborn as the
boutique Hotel Burnham
in 1999. Plush rooms are
decorated in gold and
blue, some with great
views. A complimentary
wine reception is held
every evening.

Designer Hotels

Dana Hotel & Spa
MAP K2 ▪ 660 N. State
St. ▪ 312-202-6000
▪ www.danahoteland
spa.com ▪ $
Chic and contemporary,
this boutique hotel
features rooms with
modern furnishings, floor-
to-ceiling windows, Wi-Fi,
a state-of-the-art sound
system, fine linens, and a
double-sized shower.
Guests can enjoy a range
of services available at
the spa, while the hotel
restaurant, Ajasteak,
provides a delectable
range of Asian dishes.

The James
MAP L2 ■ 55 E. Ontario St. ■ 312-337-1000 ■ www.jameshotels.com/chicago ■ $
Modern and sleek, The James feels like a home away from home. Rooms have comfortable platform beds, a small dining area, plasma TVs, stereos with MP3 docks, free Wi-Fi, and marble bathrooms.

Godfrey Hotel Chicago
MAP K2 ■ 127 W. Huron St. ■ 312-649-2000 ■ www.godfreyhotelchicago.com ■ $$
Housed in a new high-rise in trendy River North, the Godfrey offers considerable social appeal via its rooftop lounge, partially glassed-in for four-season service, with a video wall and fire pit. Its 221 rooms are loft-like and amenities include a spa and Italian restaurant.

Hard Rock Hotel
MAP L2 ■ 230 N. Michigan Ave. ■ 312-345-1000 ■ www.hardrockhotelchicago.com ■ $$
This extravagant 381-room, musically themed hotel occupies the Carbide and Carbon building – an Art Deco creation of 1929. Piped music and memorabilia are everywhere, and rooms are stylish but fun.

Hotel Allegro
MAP J4 ■ 171 W. Randolph St. ■ 312-236-0123 ■ www.allegrochicago.com ■ $$
Designer Cheryl Rowley has combined classic Art Deco features with contemporary colors and textures to great effect at this vibrant,

musically themed hotel. Complimentary wine is offered nightly to guests.

Radisson Blu Aqua Hotel Chicago
MAP L3 ■ 221 N. Columbus Dr. ■ 312-565-5258 ■ www.radissonblu.com ■ $$
In the undulating Aqua Tower, the 334-room Radisson Blu Aqua gives guests access to extensive amenities, including indoor and outdoor pools. The hotel's useful app offers a tour of its extensive art collection.

Soho House Chicago
MAP H4 ■ 113 N. Green St. ■ 312-521-8000 ■ www.sohohousechicago.com ■ $$
Belonging to the stylish Soho House clubs, the Chicago branch occupies a 19th-century factory marrying refined and raw materials, such as exposed brick walls and chandeliers. Guests have access to a members-only rooftop bar and pool, private lounge, and gym.

Thompson Chicago
MAP K1 ■ 21 E. Bellevue Pl. ■ 312-266-2100 ■ www.thompsonhotels.com ■ $$
In a good location in the Gold Coast area, the 247-room Thompson Chicago manages to make this bland high-rise engaging, through organic materials and intriguing art. Window-walled rooms, the higher the better, offer skyline views. One of Chicago's best chefs, Paul Kahan, runs the excellent Nico Osteria here, as well as the cocktail bar in the convivial lobby.

Virgin Hotels Chicago
MAP L3 ■ 203 N. Wabash Ave. ■ 312-940-4400 ■ www.virginhotels.com ■ $$
Sir Richard Branson has reinvented this hotel with good design and humor. Rooms feature sliding doors between the foyer and bedroom and ceramic dogs indicate pet-friendly rooms. Eat and drink in the first-floor diner or rooftop bar.

W Chicago Lakeshore
MAP M3 ■ 644 N. Lake Shore Dr. ■ 312-943-9200 ■ www.wchicago-lakeshore.com ■ $$
A Zen water wall and "Leave me alone," rather than "Do not disturb," signs are indications of the W's hip take on the hotel experience.

Business Hotels

Courtyard by Marriott Chicago Downtown
MAP K3 ■ 30 E. Hubbard St. ■ 312-329-2500 ■ www.courtyard.com ■ $
Bright, modern rooms with high-speed Internet access, a spacious work area, and an extra sofa-bed make this centrally located hotel a popular choice among leisure and business travelers alike.

Hyatt Regency McCormick Place
MAP D5 ■ 2233 S. Martin Luther King Jr. Dr. ■ 312-567-1234 ■ www.mccormickplace.hyatt.com ■ $
Linked by a connecting walkway to McCormick Place convention center, the basic but modern rooms of the 32-story Hyatt Regency are an

attractive stopover for conventioneers. The hotel also has a fitness facility.

Residence Inn Chicago Downtown
MAP K4 ■ 11 S. LaSalle St. ■ 312-223-8500 ■ www. marriott.com ■ $
In a historic building in downtown the Loop, this extended-stay hotel offers more style than most in the category. Rooms are spacious and come with kitchens. Amenities include a fitness center and free Wi-Fi.

Embassy Suites Hotel O'Hare-Rosemont
5500 N. River Rd., Rosemont ■ 1-847-678-4000 ■ www.embassy ohare.com ■ $$
This hotel's seven-story garden atrium makes a pleasant retreat from the hustle and bustle. Suites have all the necessary facilities; cooked breakfasts and an airport shuttle are complimentary.

Hyatt Regency Chicago
MAP L3 ■ 151 E. Wacker Dr. ■ 312-565-1234 ■ www.chicagoregency. hyatt.com ■ $$
A lobby full of greenery and fountains welcomes guests into this large hotel. Although all guest rooms offer high-speed Internet access, you can opt for a "Business Plan" upgrade to obtain more specific benefits.

Sheraton Chicago Hotel & Towers
301 E. North Water St. ■ 312-464-1000 ■ www.sheraton chicago.com ■ $$
The large, stylish guest rooms here offer fantastic

lake, city, or river views. The hotel has a business center, boat dock, health club, and five restaurants.

Swissôtel
MAP L3 ■ 323 E. Wacker Dr. ■ 312-565-0565 ■ www.swissotel.com ■ $$
Rising up where the Chicago River and Lake Michigan meet is this dramatic glass-and-steel creation. Oversized rooms contain every convenience for the business traveler and provide stellar views across the city skyline.

Westin Chicago River North
MAP K3 ■ 320 N. Dearborn St. ■ 312-744-1900 ■ www. westinchicago.com ■ $$
This sleek, four-star venue is home to a state-of-the-art Executive Business Center, fitness facility, and guest rooms featuring the comfortable Westin Heavenly Bed.

Budget Accommodation

AC Hotel Chicago
MAP L2 ■ 630 N. Rush St. ■ 312-981-6600 ■ www. marriott.com ■ $
Neutral rooms are calm, cool, and refined in this Gold Coast hotel. The lounge offers a pleasant space to start or end your evening, the restaurant serves breakfast only, and the fitness facilities include an indoor pool.

Best Western River North
MAP K3 ■ 125 W. Ohio St. ■ 312-467-0800 or 1-800-727-0800 ■ www.river northhotel.com ■ $
The location of this hotel, a little east of

the Magnificent Mile, is excellent. Rooms are spacious, with free high-speed Internet access, in-room movies, and 30 minutes of local calls. There are also parking, fitness rooms, and an indoor pool.

Freehand Chicago
MAP L3 ■ 19 E Ohio St. ■ 312-940-3699 ■ www. thefreehand.com ■ $
The stylish Freehand bills itself as a hostel, and offers shared rooms, but it also acts as a budget hotel and has small private rooms with their own bathrooms. Furthermore, its chic cocktail lounge and restaurant attract locals as well as travelers.

Hampton Inn Chicago Downtown
MAP K3 ■ 33 W. Illinois St. ■ 312-832-0330 ■ www. hamptonsuiteschicago. com ■ $
Located in River North, the Hampton Inn offers good value just a block from the Magnificent Mile. Amenities include an indoor pool, fitness center, outdoor patio, free breakfast, and complimentary Wi-Fi. The on-site restaurant Joe Fish features Italian food.

Hostelling International Chicago
MAP L5 ■ 24 E. Congress Pkwy. ■ 312-360-0300 ■ www.hichicago.org ■ $
This place is great value if you don't mind sleeping in a basic dormitory with local students. You don't need to be a member in order to stay here. The facilities include lounges, fully equipped kitchens, and bed linen.

For a key to hotel price categories see p116

Index

Acknowledgments

Authors

Chicago-based freelancer Elaine Glusac specializes in travel writing for an array of publications including *National Geographic Traveler* and the *International Herald Tribune*.

Elisa Kronish ia a Chicago native who has written about the city's highlights and hidden finds for a varity of print and online travel guides such as Citysearch Chicago.

Roberta Sotonoff is a travel junkie. She writes about a variety of travel destinations, and her work has appeared worldwide in more than 40 newspapers, magazines, online sites, and guidebooks.

Publishing Director Georgina Dee

Publisher Vivien Antwi

Design Director Phil Ormerod

Editorial Michelle Crane, Rachel Fox, Sally Schafer, Jackie Staddon, Sophie Wright

Design Tessa Bindloss, Richard Czapnik, Stuti Tiwari Bhatia

Commissioned Photography Alessandra Santarelli and Joeff Davis, Andrew Leyerle, Rough Guides/Greg Roden, Jim Warych

Picture Research Susie Peachey, Ellen Root, Lucy Sienkowska, Oran Tarjan

Cartography Subhashree Bharti, Suresh Kumar, James Macdonald, Alok Pathak

DTP Jason Little, George Nimmo

Production Olivia Jeffries

Factchecker Lauren Viera

Proofreader Susanne Hillen

Indexer Rohan Bolton

Illustrator Lee Redmond

First edition created by Departure Lounge, London

Revisions Team
Rada Radojicic, Akshay Rana, Stuti Tiwari Bhatia

Picture Credits

The publisher would like to thank the following for their kind permission to reproduce their photographs:

Key: a-above; b-below/bottom; c-centre; f-far; l-left; r-right; t-top

123RF.com: Radomír Režný 26-7.

4Corners: SIME/Gabriele Croppi 2tl, 8-9.

Adler Planetarium: 96tl.

Alamy Stock Photo: A.F. Archive 41tr, 48tr, 49cra; age fotostock/Alan Copson 1b, /Steve Dunwell 82br; Felix Choo 24cla; Ian Dagnall 64b; Danita Delimont//Russell Gordon 29c, /Alan Klehr 102-3;

Craig M. Eisenberg 28cr; Richard Ellis 55cc; Gino's Premium Images 10c; Glowimages RM 86tl; Kim Karpeles 36b, National Museum of Mexican Art 44crb, 44cl; Jason Lindsey 61tr; LOOK Die Bildagentur der Fotografen GmbH/Franz Marc Frei 59b; MARKA /Patrick Frilet 95tr; Cathyrose Melloan 16c; National Geographic Creative/ Richard Nowitz 81cl; Nikreates 4b, 11bl, 37tr; North Wind Picture Archives 40tl; PF-(bygone1) 23cb; Philip Scalia/ *Unity Temple* by Frank Lloyd Wright © ARS, NY and DACS, London 2016 36-7; Pictorial Press Ltd 40crb; Scott B. Rosen 4cl; Henryk Sadura 23b; Helen Sessions 24br, /*Crown Fountains* by Jaume Plensa © DACS 2016 34cla, 82cl; Don Smetzer 87crb; Tribune Content Agency LLC/McClatchy 67tr; Michael Ventura 17tr; ZUMA Press, Inc. 48br.

Art Effect: 90c.

Photography © The Art Institute of Chicago: 16b; *The Child's Bath* 1893) by Mary Cassatt. Oil on canvas. 100.3 x 66.1 cm (39 1/2 x 26 in.) Robert A. Waller Fund 15bl; *Nighthawks* (1942) by Edward Hopper, Oil on canvas. 33 1/8 x 60 in. (84.1 x 152.4 cm). Friends of American Art Collection. 14cla; *Two Sisters (On the Terrace)* (1881) by Pierre Auguste Renoir. Oil on canvas. 39 9/16 x 37 7/8 in. (100.5 x 81 cm) Mr. and Mrs. Lewis Larned Coburn Memorial Collection 16tl; *At the Moulin Rouge* (1892/95) by Henri de Toulouse-Lautrec. Oil on canvas. 48 7/16 x 55 1/2 in. (123 x 141 cm) Helen Birch Bartlett Memorial Collection. 15t; *American Gothic* (1930) by Grant Wood. Friends of American Art Collection 14cb.

Buddy Guy's Legends: Anthony Moser 57tr;Aaron Porter 98b.

Chicago Shakespeare Theater: James Steinkamp 54b.

The Chicago Symphony Orchestra: Todd Rosenburg Photography 75b.

Choose Chicago: Adam Alexander Photography 4cra, 47br, 52tr, 57clb, 59cra, 65tr, 66tr, 70cla, 76t; City of Chicago 28cla, 88b, /Burnham & Root 72cl, /Patrick L. Pyszka 67cl, 84-5; Patrick L. Pyszka 66b, Brian Schilling 11clb.

Corbis: Arcaid/Jon Miller/Hedrich Blessing 54tl; imageBROKER/Uwe Kazmaier 32-3; Zuma Press/ Nancy Stone 101br.

The Door: Eric Kleinberg 83c.

Dreamstime.com: Adeliepenguin 12-3; Americanspirit 12bl, 42br; Bambi L. Dingman 97cl; Thomas Barrat 50tl; Benkrut 36c; Blanscape 101br; Noah Browning 80tl; Bryan Busovicki 3tl, 68-9; Cafebeanz Company 88tr, 102cla; Cammelloribelle 80c; Clio85 34br; Cmlndm 6br, 94cra; Demerzel21 2tr, 38-9, 74clb; F11photo 35br, 46tl, 74tl; Alexandre Fagundes De Fagundes 33tl; Eugene Feygin 12cla; Cao Hai 11crb, 33bl; Jillian Cain 34-5; Kan1234 13br; Grzegorz Kieca 72bl Jessica Kirsh 73cl; Jesse Kraft 3tr, 106-7; Lightpainter 87t; Charlene C. Love 7cr; Maisna 65cl; Marchello74 4t; Mramos7637 32bl; Glenn Nagel 51cr, 62cl; Rhbabiak13 4cla; Michael Rosebrock 6cla;

Rudi1976 10cl, 71tr; Shutterfree Llc/R. Gino Santa Maria 4crb, 94cl; Sianamira 79b; Theresasc75 11cra, 96br; Tupungato 63cla; Vplut 35tl.

Courtesy of the **DuSable Museum of African-American History:** Dorling Kinderlsey Ltd/Santarelli Alessandra and Joeff Davis 45t.

Edible Ink PR: Stronghold Photography/Neil John Burger 91b.

Field Museum: 18cl, 18-9, 19cb; Greg Neise 10crb, 19tr, 19br.

Foodseum: 75cr.

Getty Images: Timothy Hiatt 64tl; Museum of Science and Industry Chicago 23tl; Scott Olson 63br; Helen H. Richardson 92tl; UniversalImagesGroup 43tl; The Washington Post/Brett T. Roseman 90tr.

Half Acre Beer Company: Beer Bokeh 92crb.

Hogsalt Hospitality: California Clipper 57br.

iStockphoto.com: stevegeer 24-5.

John G. Shedd Aquarium: Brenna Hernandez 53b.

Lincoln Park Zoo: 11cr, 30cla; Greg Neise 30-1, 31br; Todd Rosenberg Photography 30crb, 30br.

Museum of Science and Industry, Chicago, Il: 20-1, 21cr, 22tl, 53cr; J.B. Spector 10bl, 20cl, 20bl, 21tl.

Navy Pier, Inc: Nick Ulivieri 11tl.

North Pond Restaurant: 93cr.

One Off Hospitality Group, LTD: Jetel Fogelson 83tr; Chloe List 60bc.

The Promontory: 105r, Clayton Hauck 105clb.

Rex by Shutterstock: Courtesy Everett Collection 43br; KPA/Zuma 41bl; Paramount/Everett 49b; Universal Images Group/Universal History Archive 41tl.

The Richard H. Driehaus Museum: John Faier 4clb, 25bc.

Robert Harding Picture Library: Amanda Hall 79tr, 89cl; Henryk Sadura 48clb; Michael Weber 28-9.

Rosa's Lounge: 56tl.

Seminary Co-op Bookstore: Hedrich Blessing/ Steve Hall 104t.

Thomas Hart Shelby- Goat Rodeo Productions: 77cra.

Ukrainian Institute of Modern Art: 45c.

Wagstaff Worldwide: Galdones Photography/ Spiaggia Restaurant 60cr.

Willis Tower/FleishmanHillard: 7tl, 71br.

Cover

Front and spine: **Alamy Stock Photo:** Ian Dagnall. Back: **Dreamstime.com:** Benkrut.

Pull Out Map Cover

Alamy Stock Photo: Ian Dagnall.

All other images © Dorling Kindersley. For further information see: www.dkimages.com

As a guide to abbreviations in visitor information blocks: **Adm** *= admission charge;* **DA** *= disabled access*

DK | Penguin Random House

Printed and bound in China

First published in Great Britain in 2004 by Dorling Kindersley Limited 80 Strand, London WC2R 0RL

Copyright 2004, 2017 © Dorling Kindersley Limited

A Penguin Random House Company

17 18 19 20 10 9 8 7 6 5 4 3 2 1

Reprinted with revisions 2006, 2008, 2010, 2012, 2014, 2017

ISBN 978 0 2412 5964 1

MIX
Paper from responsible sources
FSC™ C018179
www.fsc.org

Selected Street Index

Chicago's Grid System

Nearly all streets in Chicago run east–west or north–south. The zero point is at the intersection of Madison Street (running east–west) and State Street (running north–south). All streets are labelled in relation to this point: for example, the section of State Street north of Madison is known as North State Street. Numbering also begins at the zero point and odd numbers are on the east sides of north–south streets and the south sides of east–west streets.